*How to Write
and Deliver
a Speech*

How to Write and Deliver a Speech

by John Ott

 Trident Press ▪ **New York**

SBN: 671-27061-3

*Library of Congress
Catalog Card Number: 76-119494*

Copyright, ©, 1970, by John Ott

*Published simultaneously in the United States and
Canada by Trident Press, a division of Simon &
Schuster, Inc., 630 Fifth Avenue, New York, N.Y.
10020*

Printed in the United States of America

Contents

Preface   7
Introduction   11

PART I   *At Your Desk*

1 : The Nature of the Beast   17
   Why a Speech?
   What Is a Speech?
   Summary

2 : Before You Write   35
   Your Approach
   Your Thesis
   Your Theme
   Random Notes
   Research at Last
   Where To Look
      GENERAL REFERENCE WORKS
      TRADE ASSOCIATIONS AS A
         SOURCE
      THE U.S. GOVERNMENT
   Your Initial Outline
   Your Working Outline
   Review Your Outline
   Summary and Checklist

3 : Sitting Down to Write   55
   Grammar
   Your Speech Consists of Words
      ACTIVE WORDS
      THE VIVID VERB
      THE DEAD PHRASE
   Common Word Traps
      THE TIRED CLICHÉ
      REDUNDANCIES AND OTHER
         IRRELEVANCIES
      THE BIG WORD
      JARGON, PROFESSIONAL AND
         OTHERWISE
   The Opening
   Get to the Point
   The Transition
   The Tone of Your Speech
      WORDS CAN CHANGE
      SPEAK SOFTLY
      CHANGE YOUR PACE
      HUMOR
   Get Involved
      THE PASSIVE VOICE
      THE OUTSIDE AUTHORITY
      STATISTICS

The Climax
The Ending
Invite Criticism
Summary and Checklist

**4 : Speeches for Most
   Occasions**   **76**
   Your Occupation
      A BUSINESS OCCASION
      A CHURCH OR SOCIAL GROUP
      A SERVICE ORGANIZATION
      YOUNG PEOPLE
   Your Interests or Hobbies
   Community Affairs
      A NEUTRAL AUDIENCE
      A GENERALLY SYMPATHETIC
         AUDIENCE
      A HOSTILE AUDIENCE

The Ceremonial Speech
Summary

**5 : Ghostwriting Is a Scary
   Business**   **94**
   Getting the Assignment
   The Interview
      GET THE FACTS
      FIND A FOCUS
      STAY IN THE BACKGROUND
      THE NEXT STEP
   Your Second Interview
   Writing for Another Voice
   The Final Draft
   Criticism
   Setting Him Up
   Summary and Checklist

PART II   *On Your Feet*

6 : Before You Speak   **111**
   Know Your Hall
   Know the People
   Your Props
   The Importance of Rehearsal
   To Read or Not to Read
   How Do You Like It Typed?
   Last-Minute Insurance
   Checklist

7 : The Perils and Pitfalls **125**
   Stage Fright
   Irrational or Just Unrealistic?
   Can You Learn to Use Fear?

Tension
Tight Throat and Stiff Jaw
*Your Voice and How It's
   Produced*
Diction

8 : Your Performance   **137**
   Mannerisms
   Use Your Personality
   Your Appearance
   *But What Do I Do with My
      Hands?*
   Your Voice
   Change of Pace

PART III   *Through the Mill*

**9 : The Ten-Minute Ordeal
   of George Morris**   **153**
Afterword   **191**

Preface

I started out honestly enough. I was a writer on the house magazine of a large corporation. I reported events the editorial staff thought would be of interest to employees. A nice job.

Then one day one of our top brass agreed to make a speech. This, in itself, was unusual because our executives never made any public appearances. I don't know if they were shy or if it was just that no one had ever asked them. In any event, this one was asked, and he accepted.

My editor gave me the job of writing the man's talk because I was the only one on his staff without an assignment at the time. There was no use in pleading that I had never written a speech. Nobody else had either.

I wrote the speech. That automatically made me the corporation's official speech writer. I was experienced.

Meanwhile, in the executive dining room, it was the winter of vice-presidential discontent. One of their number had been invited to speak in public, and he had scored heavily. Certainly what old Fred could do, any one of them could do. Suddenly, we had eight vice-presidents clamoring for platforms, subject matter, and completed speeches.

I was detached from the magazine staff and given a cubbyhole of my own where I struggled to master the intricacies of my new craft. After a year, I really was experienced.

I learned that a speech is quite different from any other literary form. Words, phrases, entire paragraphs that looked just fine on paper sounded awkward and stilted when spoken. I discovered that a speech is organized in a unique fashion, that a good speech sounds deceptively easy, but that it is unexpectedly difficult to write—if you don't happen to know a few basic techniques.

Today, many years and speeches later, it is a lot easier. But I still wish that, during my apprentice days, my cubbyhole had contained a book on how to write a speech. I don't mean a book on public speaking. These will advise a speaker how to deliver an effective speech. But most of them are silent when it comes to advice on how to write one.

This book sets out to fill such a need. At the same time, in recognition of the fact that rising to speak in public can often be a traumatic experience, attention is given to the mechanics of public speaking. The first chapter of Part I tries to explain why a speech is still one of the most effective forms of communication ever devised, and what it can do for the reputation and career of the speaker. It also tries to pin down exactly what a speech is. So far as I know, no other book takes the trouble.

Chapters 2 and 3 lay down some general rules about approaching the task of writing. I should add that they are highly personal rules which I have found to be basic. You will not find advice on how to use triads ("Friends, Romans, countrymen"), nor on the value of parallel construction ("We petitioned the school board three years ago, and what was their reply?—No. We petitioned them two years ago and what was their reply?—No. We petitioned them on the same issue this year and what was their reply?—No"). You will have to rely on others to help you discover the delights of alliteration and onomatopoeia. These are unquestionably useful devices—but more for the professional speech writer than for the occasional public speaker who must write his own copy. They are tricks of the trade and not the fundamentals, which is what this book is all about.

I have found that ninety-eight percent of all speakers are faced with a fixed number of speaking situations. Details may vary, but the essentials remain constant. Chapter 4 examines most of these situations.

Chapter 5 lets you in on the closely guarded mysteries of how to ghostwrite a speech. I have included this subject because many an unwary man has been asked by his boss to whip up a speech for him to give before the Regional Sales Conference next month. If that's your problem, you've got a bigger one than you may know. But Chapter 5 just may keep your job for you.

Part II offers some observations on how to deliver a speech. I have had speeches I have labored over lovingly delivered in such a garbled fashion that I scarcely recognized my own creation. I always resent it when this happens. One other point. It has always been a source of surprise to me that highly paid executives, who are otherwise extremely competent and organized, frequently neglect the most elementary details that surround any speaking engagement. I have known them to show up at the wrong place at the wrong time, with only the foggiest notion of the people they are going to meet and the audience they are supposed to address. In Part II, the reader will find some gentle reminders on the apparently forgotten art of proper preparation.

Part III is an attempt to gather all the principles enunciated in Parts I and II and to show how they could operate in a real-life situation. The situation is, of course, totally imaginary, as it traces the attempt of an obscure office worker to fashion a ten-minute speech to be delivered before his local chamber of commerce. I recognize that Part III may lay me open to a charge of light-hearted facetiousness, but then many "how-to" books usually impress me as being a little too earnest for their own good. Besides, the advice in this section is extremely sound.

There is no Part IV. That part is up to you.

Introduction

Unless you happen to suffer from insomnia and are reading these lines at three o'clock in the morning, somewhere, someone in this country is about to make a speech.

Such a prospect may drive you to instant slumber, but there is no escaping the fact that we are a nation much given to addressing each other in a fairly formal fashion. The ritual of the after-dinner speech is practiced nightly from the chandeliered ballrooms of big-city hotels to county grange barn suppers.

There are tens of thousands of local Rotary, Lions, Kiwanis, and other service club chapters that seem to require a speaker whenever more than two members sit down to divide a chicken. Anyone who has ever attended a meeting of the school board, a community organization, or church and social club knows that oratory of some kind is a standard fixture. Add to that the number of panel speakers at business and professional meetings, and you end up, as one conservative estimate did, with the mind-boggling figure of fifty thousand speeches given every day of the year in these United States. This is exclusive, by the way, of political speeches, lectures, and sermons. They presumably are delivered by pros who do not need the advice contained in this book.

Along with creating an awesome number of glazed expressions, the depressing statistic of fifty thousand daily speeches indicates that you are going to listen to a lot of talk in the course of a long and passive career as a member of one audience or another. But since the same fifty thousand obviously can't do all the talking, the laws of probability also indicate that, at some point, you will be the one the master of ceremonies turns to when he says, "And for our next speaker, it is my pleasure to introduce. . . ."

It is sheer nonsense to protest that no one will ever ask you to speak in public. You live in a world where you are under pressure to assume civic and community responsibility. You are concerned with education, so you think about joining the local school board or becoming a member of the PTA. You're interested in the welfare of your children, so you become involved with scouting, with the Future Farmers of America, or with the YMCA. You're ambitious and want to move ahead, so you learn as much as you can about your job. As your competence grows, so does your responsibility and your authority.

These accomplishments may not rate you a spot on the eleven o'clock news, but, unless you're the meanest man in town, you will find they have led you to become an active participant in your trade or profession and in the life of your community. This may mean many things to you, but it almost certainly means that, one day, you will be tapped to make a speech.

Whether or not it is a good speech is entirely up to you. This rather self-evident fact reduces most first-time speakers to a state of near panic. "I can't do it," is the most common reaction. "I'm no speaker." What these people are envisioning, of course, is the awful moment when they have to walk, knees trembling, to the speaker's stand to address their audience. They are worrying about their platform manner, their appearance, their performance as a speaker.

What they forget is that a speech—any speech—is made up of two parts. There is no question that performance is important. An engaging, easy style will do much to put over a speech. But along with form and style there is also content. There is the speech itself, which consists of ideas properly organized and forcefully expressed by means of the written word.

A brilliant speaker, by the virtuosity of his performance, may successfully pull off a shallow speech. But even the worst speaker in the world can't entirely kill a really good speech. He can wound it grievously, but he can't kill it.

In college, I had a professor who seemed to go into a trance each time he delivered a lecture. He mumbled haltingly in a high, thin voice. He made absolutely no contact with his students, and we all had to strain to hear him. No self-respecting speech department would dream of giving him a passing grade. But his classroom was always packed because his lectures were so tightly organized and lucidly argued. Students came to hear what he had to say, not how he said it.

This is the element so many speakers tend to overlook. A speech does not start with an audience. It should start weeks earlier, with the speaker alone, staring at a blank sheet of paper, ready to compose his thoughts.

Admittedly, it is a tough job, not made any easier by the fact that very little has ever been written about it. But Part I of this book is designed to help. It will not turn you into an orator. It is not a manual on public speaking. It will not make you the darling of the banquet circuit. But what it will do is give you some common sense advice on how to organize your thoughts and words into the shape of a simple, effective speech—one that informs and perhaps even persuades your audience. It will show you, by the use of concrete examples, how to write that most elusive form of composition—a straightforward speech.

Then, when it's time to get on your feet, you'll have confidence in what you're about to say. With a good speech in your hand, you will have won more than half the battle before you even open your mouth.

Part I

At Your Desk

CHAPTER 1

The Nature of the Beast

Why a Speech?

What with books, magazines, television, radio, and films assaulting our senses with more information than we can reasonably handle, why should anyone bother to leave a comfortable office or quiet home to hear a speech? Surely if the news the speaker has to convey is so important, we could more easily read about it or watch him tell it to us over television. Is it some masochistic drive that herds us periodically together into overheated rooms to suffer through an indigestible meal in order to listen to someone drone on endlessly about "fluctuating interest rates in the European central banking system"?

For most of us, such an assignment would indeed be a chore. But for anyone concerned with foreign banking, the topic is irresistible and attendance at the meeting a must. The reason is quite simple. The foreign banker's career depends on how well he knows his subject. The speaker may not give him any information he doesn't already have, but the banker cannot, on that account, afford to miss the speech.

However, it is not only professional interest that draws an audience together. The man who's willing to walk a mile for a Camel is a dilettante compared to the dedicated hobbyist on the trail of a meaty talk on his favorite subject. The truly enthusiastic gardener will happily travel halfway across the next county to hear the latest words on "autumnal mulching of shrubs and borders."

The desire to hear the latest news from a supposed authority is one of the principal reasons for the perennial popularity of speeches and lectures. We live in a world where new developments come crowding in before the ink is dry on even the most recent book or newest magazine article. Events occur so rapidly that anyone who hopes to stay abreast of what is happening in his field of interest simply must make use of all the communications channels available to him.

And a speech has always been one of the most effective media of communications ever devised. Certainly, it is the oldest. The first travel talk was probably given by one of our caveman ancestors who had roamed into a different part of the forest in the course of a hunting expedition and later recounted his adventures to an audience gathered about the fire. Perhaps he kindled their imagination with a vivid description of what he had seen, and perhaps he instilled in them a sense of excitement and a desire to follow his footsteps.

The ability to involve people emotionally, to move them and stir them into action or push them into a new line of thinking, has always been the unique property of a good speech. That is why it remains such an important and telling form of communication. In other media, the originator is forced to transmit his message indirectly—by means of a printed page, a television script, or a reel of film. There is no direct, flesh-and-blood confrontation.

Forty years ago, when "talkies" were first introduced,

quite a few prophets predicted the end of live theater. The argument went that theater, restricted as it was to action performed in a relatively confined space, could no longer compete with the powerful sweep of motion pictures that had the freedom to roam anywhere and show anything. Theoretically it was a sound argument, but it neglected to take into account the excitement and immediacy engendered by direct contact between actor and audience.

But even in a play there are barriers between the writer and his listeners. His thoughts and ideas are entrusted to a director and a troupe of actors who, in turn, interpret them for the public. Misunderstandings frequently arise. Anyone who believes that the imagination of a playwright is directly and effortlessly transmitted to his audience should read William Gibson's *The Seesaw Log,* an entertaining account of the frustrations he underwent in communicating his ideas in the form of a play bound for production on Broadway.

The freedom to communicate directly without the intervention of any device is an extremely powerful asset. Think how often in a business or social situation you have thought to yourself, "If only I could talk to him, everything would work out." A letter isn't good enough. Even a telephone conversation can't convey the full weight of your argument. What you want is to be physically there, face to face with your man (or woman), so that you can make contact personally. In a larger group situation, it is only through a speech that you can accomplish this end.

The Greeks, and after them the Romans, prized the skilled public speaker. Any man who hoped to gain prominence was expected to be able to talk effectively before an audience. Of course, this developed out of necessity since literacy was not widespread and writing an art restricted to the few. But honors were conferred upon the fluent orator. This is equally true today.

As a young back-bencher occupying an obscure seat in

Parliament, Winston Churchill suffered agonies each time he was called upon to speak. His delivery was uncertain and, on top of that, he had an unfortunate tendency to stutter. But Churchill had been a journalist before he became a politician, and his speeches were extraordinarily well written.

They attracted notice, and soon young Churchill began his advance through party ranks. In time he overcame his speaking handicaps to become one of the most memorable public speakers of all time.

Yet Churchill was not an unknown figure before he began his climb. He had traveled widely and had written extensively about his experiences. His books were read and generally admired. But he found the road to prominence through public speaking.

Think about your own community for a moment. You will find that its spokesmen, its leaders, are usually at ease on a platform. Their form or style of public speaking may leave something to be desired, and you may even disagree with the positions they take, but nine times out of ten their ideas come through clearly and effectively.

While it is probably true they achieved their positions through ability and talent, it is equally true that their qualifications were recognized because they were willing to speak in public.

The silent man is seldom recognized. Take every opportunity to speak before an audience. If your speech is admired, you will be too. And this does not exactly harm your career, or reduce your place in the community.

What Is a Speech?

Everyone knows the difference between a novel and a play. A poem is never confused with an essay. But what exactly is a speech? A dictionary definition exists, of course, but it hardly does justice to a unique and complex form of literary composition. That is because a speech is many things.

1. *A speech is a literary composition designed to be heard rather than read.*

Put this motto on your desk when you sit down to write a speech. Look at it often and remember it. The mistake of writing for the eye instead of the ear is the most common trap that awaits the would-be speaker. Through years of reading books, short stories, and magazine articles, we have all learned to appreciate style. Quite naturally, when we ourselves write we try to emulate what we believe are the elements of good style. But speeches are written in a very peculiar style of their own. Many great speeches read badly and many bad speeches read quite well.

"The shimmering sun slipped slowly over the southern sea" is a fine descriptive sentence—on paper. But try saying it out loud without sounding like a leaky radiator.

"The development of the internal combustion engine, considered by many to be the ultimate achievement of the industrial revolution, put the world on wheels and gave millions of people mobility for the first time, allowing them an opportunity to satisfy their intellectual curiosity and enlarge their horizons."

Although a bit cumbersome, this passage is perfectly acceptable in print. The eye can grasp its meaning without any trouble. But not the ear—not unless the speaker has a pair of lungs like a set of bellows. The sentence is far too long to be read with a single breath. Besides, there's an unexpected booby trap in the words, "millions of people mobility." That's not easy to say, as an experimental reading will quickly tell you.

On the other hand: "Plough, plant, reap. Plough, plant,

reap. A cycle of hope. A wheel of fortune. A ring of despair. The greater part of mankind is tied to this endless circle." These words are meant to be heard, not read.

In 1962 President Kennedy argued for more medical care through Social Security. In describing the plight of a retired couple living on pension and Social Security checks, he used these words:

"Now therefore his basic needs are taken care of. He owns his house. He has $2,500 or $3,000 in the bank. And then his wife gets sick.

"And we're all going to be in a hospital—nine out of ten of us—before we finally pass away. And particularly when we're over sixty-five.

"Now she is sick—not just for a week but for a long time. First goes the $2,500. That's gone. Next he mortgages his house, even though he may have some difficulty making the payments out of his Social Security."

This is not a particularly elegant passage. It would win no high marks in an English composition class. But President Kennedy, who could write extremely graceful prose, chose this style as best suited to the demands of the occasion. He recognized that a debate on the merits of increased medical support for the aged could be carried out on a highly impersonal level, citing federal expenditures, budgetary requirements, and existing taxation rates. He also recognized that such an approach would probably defeat his argument. He chose, instead, to emphasize the human element, and he illustrated his point of view by sketching a very real problem in graphic and universally understandable terms. This is another attribute of a successful speech.

2. *A speech is a literary composition that uses simple, graphic, and concrete language. It avoids generalities.*

The ear dislikes generalities. It responds to clear images. If an idea is not sharply expressed in a book, the reader can always return to the sentence and examine it a second time. But there are no second chances in a speech. The speaker must make absolutely certain his audience gets the point— even at the sacrifice of what he considers to be style.

In May 1940, President Roosevelt went before both houses of Congress to make an appeal for larger defense expenditures. He was convinced that the country was in great danger. But he also recognized the isolationist mood of the time. He determined to break through this mood and sound an urgent alarm. During the course of the speech, he referred to—what was then—the relatively new danger of attack by air. He could have said:

"In a different era, when men-of-war under sail moved slowly, our first line of defense was the ocean. Even more recently, battleships still took a long time to reach our shores. But oceans are no longer a barrier. Modern aircraft can now travel vast distances in a very short time." This certainly stated the problem, but notice the lack of any specifics.

Instead, he outlined the situation this way:

"The Atlantic and Pacific Oceans were reasonably adequate barriers when fleets under sail moved at an average speed of five miles an hour. . . . Later, the oceans still gave strength to our defense when fleets and convoys propelled by steam could sail the oceans at fifteen or twenty miles an hour.

"But the new element—air navigation—steps up the speed

of possible attack to two hundred or three hundred miles an hour.

"From the fields of Greenland, it is four hours by air to Newfoundland, five hours to Nova Scotia . . . and only six hours to New England.

". . . If Bermuda fell into hostile hands, it is a matter of a little over three hours for modern bombers to reach our shores.

"From a base in the outer West Indies, the coast of Florida could be reached in two hundred minutes."

The first version was content to state the general fact that the United States was more vulnerable to attack because fire power could be directed at the country in a much shorter length of time than ever before.

The second version gave specific information on exactly how much time and distance had shrunk. The danger was not just a shorter time away than it had ever been. To be precise, it was only two hundred minutes away. There is nothing vague or uncertain about that. It is not a generality, but a graphic, unforgettable statement.

It is also stacking the cards in favor of the speaker. If you'll notice, there is nothing haphazard in the way President Roosevelt arranged the order of his figures. First, an attack was only four, five, or six hours away. In the next paragraph, it was "a little over three hours" distant. Finally, our shores could "be reached in two hundred minutes."

The sense of urgency increases with each statement. The time narrows from a matter of hours to one of minutes. And I wonder if any member of Congress noticed, as he was listening, that "two hundred minutes" is roughly equivalent to "a little over three hours."

Yes, this is a trick, but a perfectly legitimate one, because a good speech sets out to involve people emotionally.

3. *A speech is a literary composition that demands a positive response to the speaker's thesis.*

One might argue that every word ever written is designed by the author to draw a response on the part of his audience. In a sense that is true, but there are certain differences between a speech and other forms of prose composition. A speech is not an essay, an article, or a report. These are usually content to describe a certain place, event, or situation. They may dispassionately recommend a course of action or take a position. But their principal function is to lay out the facts of the matter in a concise and logical fashion. While the author's point of view undoubtedly comes through, it is essentially up to the reader to decide how he feels about the issues raised and what he wants to do about them.

While a speech must be concise and logical, it cannot be dispassionate. In preparing and making a speech, it is crucial to involve your audience's feelings. A speech is not a fair or impartial account. The effective speaker takes sides and actively urges his listeners to join in his enthusiasm or disapproval. A book or an article invites conclusions. A good speech demands them.

The reason again is time, or lack of a second chance. A speaker usually has less than thirty minutes to make his argument. His audience hears him once and only once. The article writer or book author, on the other hand, can afford to present his case in a lower key, to be more leisurely in making his points. In fact, he dare not overstate his case. Hyperbole looks ridiculous in cold print, and a reader is understandably suspicious of exaggeration. Of course, wild flights of rhetoric can destroy a speech as well, but a little verbal stretching, such as giving the impression that two hundred minutes is a much shorter time than a period of a little over three hours, is definitely within the rules.

At this point you may wonder, "Why am I being told all this? I'm not a politician or a demagogue. I'm not running for office, thank God, and I don't want to start a revolution. My problem is that I've got to get up in front of the church adults group next Wednesday and tell them about my trip to Mexico—and without slides!"

If this, indeed, is going to be your speech, you'll definitely leave them yawning. A description of the miles you traveled and the sights you took in has all the built-in excitement of a bottle of stale root beer.

Ask yourself, instead, what you really thought of Mexico. You may have hated every hour you spent there. But whether you liked it or not, use your own impressions of the country and its people as a starting point. Then your problem becomes one of persuading your audience to share your view. If you've done a good job, you'll send them home to pack their bags, or they'll write the country off any vacation plans they might have. But, one way or another, your talk will have created a very definite response on the part of your audience, and this is perhaps the single most important characteristic of a successful speech. A bland speech is a waste of everyone's time.

When a speaker stands before his audience and declares: "Life insurance is the most exciting and challenging occupation in the world," there will surely be someone in the crowd who isn't convinced. He's thought all along that Grand Prix racing is the most exciting and challenging way to make a living. But if the speaker really warms to his subject, pointing out the essential services performed by insurance salesmen, how they can change the lives of entire families, how they can mean the difference between comfort and bare survival, how they can offer greater educational and career opportunities for thousands upon thousands of young people —then perhaps the racing fan will leave the meeting with a greater appreciation of the insurance profession. He will not be won over to the speaker's statement about his own occupation, but he may think somewhat differently about the insurance man's role in life. However, if the speaker had opened his remarks by stating: "Life insurance is an extremely demanding occupation, but it has many rewards," and then went on to expand on that theme, everyone's opinion of life insurance as a pretty dull business would be thoroughly reinforced. The statement is true, of course. It is demanding and there are rewards. But then probably every member of the audience could say the same about his own job. A speaker who expounds on the obvious has clearly forgotten his audience. And a speech does not really exist without an audience to hear it.

4. *A speech is a literary composition especially designed for one particular audience.*

The President of the United States, when he delivers a major policy address on television, is directing his remarks to the entire nation. His is a broad-gauge audience that cuts across many specialized interests. Teachers, firemen, truck drivers, and camera enthusiasts all have a stake in the future of their country, and all are prepared to hear what he has to say about it. Congressmen, governors, mayors—in fact, all politicians—often speak to large groups of people with highly diverse interests. But even then they do not limit themselves to a discussion of abstract issues.

Any newspaperman covering a campaign will tell you that most politicians have a standard, set speech which they use over and over again. However, the speech will contain a number of interchangeable paragraphs that are designed to appeal to the audience of the moment.

Speaking in Iowa, a presidential candidate will invariably refer to the shockingly low prices farmers are forced to accept for their livestock and produce. In San Francisco, before a women's group, the paragraph will be changed to express indignation over the shockingly high prices housewives must pay to feed their families.

Here is an example of the interchangeable or modular paragraph: "Ladies and gentlemen, *A* has always held a special fascination for me. That is because the voters of this community have *B*. This year, I look forward to *C*. In this effort, which involves all of us, I count heavily upon the imagination and forward-looking leadership of *D*."

Insert the appropriate phrases:

A. Name of place, Kansas City, the Seventeenth District, etc.
B. 1. "always voted for the candidate of the party I represent."
   2. "never once voted for the candidate of the party I represent."
   3. "shown their independence by cutting across party lines to vote for the man rather than his party."
C. 1. "continuing this fine tradition."
   2. "winning your support and beginning a new tradition."
   3. "proving to you that I am the man who deserves your support."
D. 1. "the business community."
   2. "organized labor."
   3. "members of that unsung profession who contribute so mightily to our physical well-being—and I salute all of you who proudly call yourselves dental technicians."

As in ordering a Chinese meal, the trick is to pick one appropriate selection each from columns A, B, C, and D. With the proper choice, the candidate then has a paragraph he can use for virtually any occasion.

Men seeking public office, like most speakers, usually find themselves before an audience composed of individuals who have been drawn together because they share a common interest or purpose. If a common interest or purpose is lacking, then an audience often shares some characteristic. It may be a group of women, or a youth organization. They may all be members of the same club or fraternal order. Whatever it is, there will be some common denominator in each audience you face, and your speech should be tailored to appeal to that thread.

Let's assume you are a petroleum engineer and are asked to speak on "Modern Petroleum Technology." It would be a serious mistake for you to write your speech before inquiring carefully about the nature of your audience.

Here is how it could change, depending upon your listeners.

Members of your own profession: No definitions, no explanations. Your audience is not interested in how modern petroleum technology works. They know. Instead, you might concentrate on innovations and how they will affect the future of the profession.

A women's club: A survey of alternate methods of catalytic cracking will not delight the ladies. But they would probably be amazed at the range of petroleum derivatives that are basic to the many products they use every day. Show them that the petroleum industry means a great deal more than gas and oil for the family car.

An adult education group: If they're what they claim to be, these people are interested in how modern petroleum technology works. They don't know, and you can tell them. They should leave the meeting with some added knowledge together with a greater appreciation of a complex industry and the role it plays in their lives. But don't make it too technical.

A Rotary, Kiwanis, or other service organization: Service is the key word here. Petroleum and all the products derived from it have made enormous contributions to the welfare and progress of mankind. Measure it for them. Provide them with a fresh perspective.

This process of tailoring a rather general speech topic to appeal to the natural interests of your audience is something that cannot be neglected. The subject of "Our Crowded Highways—A Transportation Bottleneck" will not find a responsive audience among the Eskimos. The topic is simply not relevant to their lives or their problems. Once you establish an approach that is relevant to the occasion, you can then move on to a consideration of what you want your speech to accomplish.

5. *A speech is a literary composition that sets out to accomplish certain clear-cut objectives.*

Again, this might appear to be a statement of the obvious. Hopefully, every written work has an objective. Write a pointless book and you've got a failure on your hands. But the objectives of a good speech are unusually precise and well defined, far more so than in any other literary form. A good speech accomplishes one or more specific tasks and can be structured in the following ways.

To inform: The principal objective of a speech can be to inform the audience. Most lectures fall into this category. "Lighting Techniques for Indoor Color Photography" could well be the title of a speech whose main and perhaps only purpose is to provide information. A talk of this sort is generally given by an expert to an audience whose interest in the subject is avid. But the speech need not be pedantic or dull. The dynamics of such a speech involve a transfer of knowledge, but the transfer should not take place in an academically objective fashion. The subject should be presented so that the audience can barely be restrained from rushing home to try out the new expertise they have acquired. Similar excitement can and should be kindled by any speech that sets out to inform. There are, of course, exceptions. It is difficult to imagine much enthusiasm being produced by a topic like "Economic Determinism Among Laplanders." But perhaps this should be a conversation and not a speech, since it is unlikely one could ever find more than two or three people sufficiently interested in the problem.

To persuade: This is probably the most common speech of all. The object here is to convince the audience of the truth of your proposition. "Violence on Television Gives Children a Distorted View of Life" or "Why We Should Watch Our Weight" or "America's Space Program Is a Waste of Time and Money" are all examples of the genre. When an audience attends a speech with a title like any one of these, it knows exactly what to expect. All members of the audience, of course, may not agree with the proposition, but they are willing to listen. It is then up to you to persuade them to change their minds. But do it carefully. Do not offend. Do not belittle the opposition. Above all, be logical, and lard your speech with plenty of supporting facts, examples, and anecdotes. You may, if you wish, take a step beyond mere persuasion. You can design your speech to accomplish still another function.

To motivate: This type of speech states a problem, and urges the audience to take a direct and immediate course of action with respect to it. Naturally, the speech meant to persuade also assumes some form of subsequent action. Having won his listeners over to his viewpoint, the speaker expects them to respond. But in the case of the speech designed to motivate, purposeful action is demanded without delay.

The most notable examples of this sort of speech can be found in the literature of the revolution. These are the speeches that send people to the barricades. These are also, it should be noted, the speeches that provided the spark for our own War of Independence. But these statements are not the exclusive property of firebrands.

They are useful models if you ever find yourself speaking, as a member of your local school board, on behalf of urgently needed curriculum reform or a new bond issue. You may be so indignant about the bloodshed on television that you won't be content merely to convince your audience of the widespread abuses seen nightly by their children. In that event, you could talk to your local Lions Club chapter on "How We Can Stop Violence on Television—Now!"

It isn't just the gut issue that invites such a speech. I've heard a group of financial executives become positively emotional when one of their number stood up to tell them what they had to do in order to win greater freedom from what he considered to be burdensome Security Exchange Commission regulations. His speech sported the stirring title of "Financial Disclosure for the Conglomerate Corporation." When he had finished, you felt that the assembled accountants were prepared to tear up the paving stones and march in a body on Washington. They might have even done it, at that. But they'd all just had lunch.

At the other end of the spectrum from the speech that incites action is an entirely different kind of talk—one that is designed

To stimulate: The purpose of this type of address is to enrich the intellectual and emotional lives of your audience. It is not restricted to the so-called inspirational message, but embraces talks on art, music appreciation, and other related topics. Strictly, it does not include the subject of "The Art of Japanese Flower Arrangement," since this is primarily a speech meant to inform. However, "Picasso—Giant of Twentieth Century Art" would most definitely fall into this category. In the ordinary course of events, few of us will be called upon to deliver a talk of this nature, and so a longer commentary is unnecessary. Equally specialized is the speech whose intent is

To entertain: The dictionary defines this verb as "to engage the attention of." To that extent, every effective speech entertains an audience. But entertainment, pure and simple, is probably not its principal aim. The ability to deliver a truly amusing and entertaining after-dinner speech, on the other hand, is a rare quality, and the speaker capable of it is very much in demand. Mark Twain and Robert Benchley both had the knack. But they were professionals who demanded and got stiff fees for their services. A touch of humor is a valuable asset to a speech. But if you happen to get a laugh with one of your stories, don't think you're instant Bob Hope. A really good stand-up comic takes years to perfect his timing. He also has a stable of gag writers working for him, and you don't. Leave the comic speech to the pros.

Finally, there is a speech with which we are all, unfortunately, too familiar. It is a talk whose principal purpose is

To commemorate: Anniversaries, dedications, retirements, ground-breaking rites are all occasions for what I call "The Ceremonial Speech." You probably have suffered through dozens. You may have to give one tomorrow. In either case, you have my sympathy. Although they are usually (God help us if they're not) short, they are extraordinarily difficult to make interesting. However, since they are one of the speeches you will be asked to make more frequently than any other, they deserve, and are given, a separate section later in the book.

These six categories are meant to serve only as a rough catalog of the types of speech that are most commonly given. Obviously, any one speech will stray over these divisions. A speech may be designed to persuade; but it must also inform the audience of certain relevant facts that lead to the ultimate conclusion. And it would be extremely helpful if the talk managed to entertain as well.

Summary

In an attempt to answer the question "What is a speech?" the following definitions have been suggested.

A speech is a literary composition that:

1. is designed to be heard rather than read;
2. avoids generalities;
3. demands a positive response to the speaker's thesis;
4. is especially designed for one particular audience;
5. sets out to accomplish certain clear-cut objectives.

Although the definitions vary, you'll notice the repeated reference to the point that a speech is a literary composition. This means putting words down on paper. This is not as frightening as it may seem. As the next chapter will demonstrate, the rules that apply to speech writing are simple and fairly easy to remember.

CHAPTER 2

Before You Write

Your Approach

When faced with the reality of an actual assignment, the first instinct of most professional speech writers I know is to stretch out on a couch or call up a friend for lunch. It's not that they're lazier than most. The prospect of hard work affects speech writers in about the same measure as it does everyone. In any case, it's their job and they know they've got to get it done. But they have learned, usually through bitter experience, that putting a piece of paper in a type-writer and starting out headlong is possibly the very worst way to begin. They know there is no such thing as a single speech on a subject such as "The Role of Police in Civil Disorders," or even, to choose a less controversial topic, "Constructive Toys for Children." There are a number possible on each. One subject may be more inflammatory than the other, but both involve the expression of personal opinion. And, as we all know, there are as many opinions on a given subject as there are people ready to talk about it. It all depends on the speaker's views, his approach to the problem.

So the first of three related questions a professional speech writer asks himself is how to best approach the issue he is about to tackle. The more introspective members of the fraternity prefer to be alone with their thoughts, idly running over various possibilities. This is the flat-on-a-couch or feet-on-a-desk school. The more outgoing type wants a sounding board he can talk against. Hence the invitation to lunch, which, incidentally, can be unbelievably boring for the invitee. The speech writer, you see, is not really after conversation. He's simply trying out ideas, and he'd rather do it in the company of someone he knows reasonably well.

Whichever style you prefer, this is the initial step. Long before you settle down to the chore of writing your speech, consider first the approach you are going to take. Among other things, this involves a consideration of your audience. Are they intellectual heavyweights, or will you be talking to a youth group? The occasion itself has an effect on the approach you will select.

For example, the program of an annual industry association meeting in Las Vegas will contain a number of different events. There will be working sessions or seminars during the day. These call for a no-nonsense presentation, and your approach should be correspondingly businesslike. But evenings are usually given over to a reception, followed by a dinner and a main speaker. This is often an elder statesman evaluating the industry's progress during the year and providing guidelines for the future. And, at that point, who really cares? The audience down front is trapped into a polite attention. But not the boys in the back. Safe from the disapproving stare of the program chairman and aglow from too much food and drink, they are plotting their evening's fun. They've worked hard all day, and they feel they're entitled to some good times—if only the speaker would have the courtesy to wrap up his remarks and release them. I don't know why, but those who plan such functions nearly always reserve their big speaking guns for the evening banquet, thus assuring them of a minimum of attention.

I was once asked to write a speech for the executive vice-president for research and development of one of the largest technologically oriented corporations in the world. The occasion was a conference on computers and my man was to close a two-day working convention with an after-dinner speech. He was one of the most respected scientists and engineers in the country and was expected to cap the conference with appropriate words of wisdom.

I worked out a dandy speech for him entitled, "The Need for a More Viable Man-Machine Interface." It was, with all due modesty, a fairly impressive plea for computer scientists to develop a more effective way for the ordinary man in the street to use a computer. Forget about higher speeds and greater memory capacity, he was saying, and instead find a way for a businessman to communicate directly to the machine without having to go through a computer programmer or being forced to learn a new skill.

Keeping in mind that the room would be full of Ph.D.s, engineers, and other high-powered types, I drew heavily on the technical literature, and I wrote what I thought to be a most appropriate talk. He read through my draft and tossed it on the desk with an approving nod. "It's a nice job," he said. "But we're going to have to start all over."

I couldn't understand it. The speech was sound, and I was convinced the arguments were persuasive. He brushed me aside with a wave of his hand. "Sure," he said. "It's great. That's the trouble. I know these clowns. After two days of butting heads in seminars, they'll want to relax. Do me the same speech, but put a little fun in it."

That's exactly what I did. I took out all the technical jargon, played around with the ideas, and cracked some jokes.

The speech, which was now down to fifteen minutes, was an outstanding success. He had them rolling in the aisles, and they gave him a standing ovation when it was over.

A couple of months later this same man was invited to deliver a paper in Switzerland at an international convocation on computer technology. He gave the same speech, but in the original version, and it, too, was an outstanding success. The two speeches were identical in subject matter, but they were worlds apart in approach—each one perfectly suited to the occasion and to a particular audience.

Your Thesis

The thesis of a speech is what it's all about. It's your central argument or statement, the essence of what you want to convey to your audience. It is surprising how many would-be speakers never get around to their main point. How often have you heard speakers who talk in circles, occasionally edging closer to the heart of the matter, then backing away erratically? This all too common fault can be eliminated, provided you ask yourself early in the game, "What do I want to say?"

In the case of my executive VP for research and development, the process went something like this. There was no question about the general topic. It had to be on some aspect of computer technology. But this is a vast subject. What did he want to say about computer technology? How it's revolutionized business? Everybody knew that. It had been talked to death. How it has dramatically changed the way we all live? Better. The field had been worked over pretty hard but maybe something new could be uncovered. How the computer was going to revolutionize life even more in the future than it has in the past? Better still. Everybody enjoys a look into the future and science fiction is always fun. Then a simple question was asked. "If you had to choose, what single new development in computer technology would have the greatest impact on our society?"

There were a number of possible answers, of course. Make them bigger; make them cheaper; make them more widely available to developing countries. The list grew. At last we came up with an answer that satisfied him and intrigued me. And here was the thesis of his speech:

"If we can find a way to make the computer as simple to operate as the telephone, the impact on our society will be more profound than any other technological development ever conceived by man."

Well now, that's a big statement. A writer can play with that. It's either true or it isn't. There was a question naturally whether the speech could support such a thesis. But that's not really the point here. The important achievement was that we had hammered out the central statement of his speech. We had our thesis. We knew where we were going, or rather where we wanted to go. Subsequent research and writing would determine if we would ever get there.

Your Theme

The theme of a speech is the manner in which you present your thesis. It is the tone and texture of your speech, your view of the thesis you have stated. What are the consequences of making the computer more universally available? Do you view such a development with alarm, or do you find it an exciting prospect? Are you going to warn your audience of the inherent dangers, or are you going to stir them up by outlining the possibilities ahead? When you deal with questions such as these, you are working out a theme for your speech.

Very few speeches, of course, are built around a single

theme. As in a musical composition, variations on a central theme are not only possible, they are desirable. But keep in mind that they should bear a relationship to your main point of view. In the case of the computer speech, my man was essentially up-beat about the consequences of his thesis. He thought it was a desirable development, and we painted a rather exciting picture of what life would be like with a computer terminal in every home and office. We speculated on how it would change the quality of everyday life, and how it could lead to general improvements in terms of greater efficiency and increased leisure time. But—and here the theme changed and took on a darker tone—we warned that such an increase in leisure time created its own problems. Would people learn to fill it productively, or would it, in fact, become a burden? Then, after discussing some of these negative aspects, we returned to the central theme—that it was a great idea, holding out the promise of brand new opportunities and rewards that deserved to be explored.

Each section of a speech, from opening paragraph to final conclusion, should be prepared with a definite theme in mind. Otherwise, your audience may not understand *your* views on the subject under discussion. And this, after all, is what they have come to hear. They will not be moved by a recitation of facts. They want to know how you feel.

To be absolutely candid, at this early stage there is little to be gained by attempting to establish a theme for every part of your speech. This will slowly evolve as you prepare your outline. However, it is important to plant your overall theme clearly in your own mind.

As I mentioned earlier, the three questions of approach, thesis, and theme are related. To a certain extent each depends on the other, and to a larger extent all depend upon the nature of your audience and the occasion at which you will be speaking. Consider each one of them carefully. Decide early in the game what each one will be, and you will keep yourself and your audience from floundering about unnecessarily. Establishing these unmistakably will also make your job much easier later on.

Random Notes

Research is an essential ingredient in any speech. It is vital that you base your thesis and theme on a solid bedrock of factually correct information. Despite the performance of some of our better-known speakers, especially those in politics, speeches are not works of fantasy. They rest on facts, so dig for them you must. But research, badly done, can be a trap. The principal reason for this is an overabundance of material. No matter what your subject, there is likely to be an entire library shelf of books and periodicals devoted to exploring every corner of it. Buried in this mountain of data is the information you want. But how do you dig it out?

Some people never learn. For a number of years, I worked next door to a fellow speech writer who was a compulsive researcher. The corporation was a large one, and he wrote speeches for the chairman of the board, who had become a national and even international figure, partly on the basis of speeches my friend wrote for him. Clearly my neighbor was experienced in his craft, and extremely competent. But researching a speech was pure hell for him—and for the research staff that worked with him.

I always knew when he was fresh on a new assignment. A never-ending parade of office boys bringing him books, papers, and magazines heralded this event as surely as the first robin heralds spring. At these times, whenever I dropped by for a chat he would be on the telephone, in pursuit of another scrap of information, hastily scribbling notes on stray pieces of paper which he would subsequently lose. My God, how that man took notes! I have seen him leave for the weekend with two suitcases bulging with reading files, only to return on Monday eager to attack a fresh pile of paper.

Only after collecting enough background to satisfy William Jennings Bryan, who I understand seldom took less than several hours on the platform, would my friend sit down to prepare the outline for a twenty-minute talk. Naturally, he had far too much material. The result was that he was forced to undergo an even more agonizing time. He had to discard much of what he had laboriously gathered together, and he hated to see any of it go. It was not an easy process for him or for the rest of us, and it grew increasingly desperate as his deadline approached.

I felt at the time that there had to be an easier way, and I still think so. My answer has always been to make random notes. This looks a great deal like idle doodling and so is open to suspicion from one's boss, but I have found it worthwhile. My method is to write down my thesis on a note pad, and then speculate on what kind of information I might need to support it. I have long since thrown away my notes for the computer speech. But if I were to write it today, here are some of the jottings I would make to myself.

1. Has anything ever been written on the subject? Find out.

2. What about the technology? Is it possible, or is it in the realm of science fiction? Collect important papers on how people use computers.

3. Is it any easier today to use a computer than it was ten years ago? If so, how?

4. Is the proposition economically possible, or is it financially out of sight?

5. What about comparing the proliferation of telephone technology to that associated with computers? Crazy idea? Ask.

The list would go on, but the point should be clear. Random notes help you begin to crystallize your own thoughts. They help focus on the kind of research you must do in order to get the information you must have.

Research at Last

Productive research is not the indiscriminate collection of data that falls under the general heading of your topic. It is the ability to separate meaningful information from facts. And by meaningful, I mean meaningful to you. It may be a fact that computers have saved chain stores millions of dollars in achieving much tighter inventory control. But does that fact have any bearing on the thesis of my speech, namely, that making computers more widely available to individuals will have a profound impact on our society? Probably not. But an article pointing out that the industry is now spending more money on peripheral equipment than it is on computers themselves is of great interest. If I am going to write such a speech, I will want a copy of that article.

A thorough review of your approach, theme, and thesis, together with an analysis of your random notes, will help you develop a direction for your research. Before you begin to collect information, make a list of what kind of information you're looking for. I realize that not many occasional speech writers are blessed with the resources of a professional editorial research staff. I have been reasonably fortunate in this respect, and I have learned some invaluable tips from them.

I vividly remember one infinitely patient lady in a government bureau in Washington who was asked to help me with a speech I had to write on education in the South. I was pretty young at the time, and I approached her with an innocent request for any information she might have on the subject.

"Honey," she said with a resigned sigh, "I've got rooms and rooms of everything that's ever been written about education in the South. Just what did you want to know about it?"

Her question stopped me cold. What *did* I want to know about the subject? I stammered about for a while, obviously not clear in my own mind what it was I needed. At last she stopped me with a kindly pat on my arm. "You go on home and think about it," she said. "And when you've got it worked out, I'll be right here."

It was sensible advice. I thought through my speech and managed to zero in on what I thought would be key areas. Sure enough, when I was able to tell her more or less precisely what I wanted, it was on my reading desk within fifteen minutes. Research, whether you do it yourself or use an assistant, should be directed to be productive. Another rule about research is this: too little is probably more than enough, and too much just clogs the machinery. Besides, you'll find, if you've planned your research at all carefully, that a few well-chosen sources will suggest more and, generally, they'll be on target for what you need.

Where To Look

Having taken these preliminary steps, where do you look? What are the standard sources for research? I suggest that you begin with your local library. The process is disarmingly simple and surprisingly painless. You merely go up to the reference desk if your library is big enough to have one, or to the nearest official-looking type behind a counter if it isn't, and present your problem. Explain that you want information on your problem, and outline the kind of background you're looking for.

The chances are that your local librarian, who has probably had an expensive education and possesses a master's degree in library science, will go numb for a moment until she gets over her initial shock. It's quite likely that no one has asked her such a question since her university days. For years, all she's been doing is cataloging books and stamping them in and out. At last, you're giving her an opportunity to use the skills for which she was trained. The service and the cooperation you will get will very likely amaze and gratify you.

However, if you prefer to do it yourself, here are a few standard sources.

GENERAL REFERENCE WORKS

Any of the encyclopedias. They may not be too helpful, but if the article is signed, note the author's name and consult the card catalog. He wrote it because he's an authority in his field and he probably has written other books on the subject. Almanacs can be handy, too. They contain all sorts of statistical information. Two of the very best sources are *Reader's Guide to Periodical Literature,* which lists, by subject, most of the magazine articles ever published in the United States, and the *New York Times Index,* which does the same for that newspaper. Then you can write for reprints, or perhaps your library has copies or microfilm.

TRADE ASSOCIATIONS AS A SOURCE

Whether it's beekeeping or stamp collecting, glass blowing or the manufacture of clarinets, there is virtually always a trade group or an association of enthusiasts who have banded together and publish literature on their subject. Ask your librarian to help you locate the organization and write to it. You're almost certain to get more than you need.

The U.S. Government Printing Office must be the largest printer in the world. Our federal agencies put out a river of pamphlets and brochures on an unbelievably wide variety of subject matter. The Printing Office has a catalog, and your librarian will surely have a copy.

Finally, there's the face-to-face interview. If you have to speak on a technical subject, or on one on which you are relatively uninformed, find out who the experts are. Most experts love to be consulted. If you can't see them, write them a letter requesting sources of information. In most cases, they'll be flattered and will put you on the right track.

These sources I have mentioned are all useful as starting points. You will find, as you go more deeply into your subject, that you will uncover many others—certainly enough to build a formidable pile of material from which you can construct your outline.

Your Initial Outline

The outline of your speech is your road map. It tells you where you're going, and it reminds you where you've been so that you don't repeat yourself. It is also a guarantee that you will proceed with your principal points in a logical manner. The preparation of a good working outline for your speech is perhaps the most critical phase of the entire writing process. Here is where most speeches tend to go astray, resulting in poor organization and fuzzy thinking. Rhetoric alone does not make a good speech. What is needed, above all, is a strong, forceful arrangement of your statements and your arguments.

Since speeches are on all sorts of different subjects, no two outlines are alike. But there is a general principle that should be followed. Think your entire speech through from thesis to conclusion and list the major points you intend to stress. As an example, let's take a speech subject mentioned earlier: "Violence on Television Gives Children a Distorted View of Life." Bearing in mind that I want the audience to take an active role with respect to this problem, I would organize my initial outline as follows:

1. Opening.
2. State the problem.
3. Prove the existence of the problem.
4. Describe the consequences of the problem.
5. Show how these consequences affect the audience and persuade them to become concerned.
6. Pose the central question: Is there a solution?
7. State the solution.
8. Document why this would be the most effective solution.
9. Relate the audience to the proposed solution; why they should support it.
10. A call to action; how they can support it.
11. Conclusion. The result of their action. The beneficial change and advantages of supporting the proposal with the suggested action.

This, of course, is hardly a working outline. However now, because I know roughly where I'm going, I can become more detailed.

Your Working Outline

A highly detailed working outline is extremely useful for those who find they are self-conscious and stiff when they begin to put what they hope are finished words on paper. With an outline, you can convince yourself that style doesn't really count. You can be relaxed and easy. As an added advantage, when you've finished it you may find, to your surprise, that you've practically written your speech. As an exercise let's expand the previous initial outline into a full-fledged working one, and you'll see what I mean. Putting aside the opening, which presents very special problems of its own, and which will be discussed later, here is how it would look:

1. Opening.
2. State the problem:
   a. Find an anecdote that clearly illustrates the major point. Is there in the research material an example of a youngster who behaved in real life in a violent manner because he admitted he had seen it done that way on television and therefore believed that this was the universal custom?
   b. His behavior is hardly surprising when you consider that impressionable young minds are exposed daily to situations where violence seems normal. Find a statement by a child psychologist or expert in mental health that supports the view that the behavior of a child is more influenced by what he sees in the world around him than by what he learns formally in school.
   c. If this is true, what does he see? How many hours a day does the average child watch television?
3. Prove the existence of the problem:
   a. Find statistics citing the number of acts of violence that are committed daily, weekly, monthly, or yearly on television.
   b. Describe the variety of these acts from simple assault to murder. Include those that can be interpreted as encouraging a sadistic pleasure in inflicting pain or bodily injury. Make this as strong as possible. Statistics here are going to be impressive.
   c. Try to find a quote from a prominent educator or

some other authority who sat in front of a television set for a week and listed all the different kinds of violence he saw. This reinforces the statistics and gives them credibility.

d. What is the net effect of all this on the child and his behavior? Locate specific examples of what a number of children did as a direct consequence of having seen it on television.

e. Go from the specific to the general. Get quotes from those concerned indicating the scope of the problem. These must be from authorities. The more urgent the better. Establish without question that a serious and widespread problem exists.

4. Describe the consequences of the problem:

a. Beyond the immediate problem of childhood behavior, how does early exposure to violence affect later adult behavior? Try to find an example of a convicted criminal who admits to a relationship between early TV violence fantasies and subsequent actions. If this is not possible, search for quotes by psychologists, sociologists, or police authorities. Surely some correlation exists.

b. Wrap up this section by stating that the consequences result in:

(1) Antisocial behavior in childhood.

(2) A greater likelihood of antisocial behavior as an adult.

c. Add up what this costs in terms of:

(1) Property value.

(2) Human values.

(3) Wasted lives.

(4) Loss to society both in human and material resources.

5. Show how these consequences affect the audience and persuade them to become concerned:

a. Previous section leads directly into relating the audience with the problem.
   (1) Their property could be destroyed or damaged.
   (2) Their personal welfare could conceivably be threatened.
   (3) Ask them how many hours their own children watch TV.
   (4) Ask if they monitor what their children watch. Have they counted the number of violent acts their children are exposed to?
   (5) Suggest strongly that their own kids could easily develop a warped view because of this exposure.
6. Pose the central question: Is there a solution?
   a. Ask the audience if they want to run this kind of risk.
   b. Ask if they think there is a solution.
   c. Convince them that one must be found.
7. State the solution:
   a. Describe what steps can be effective in limiting television violence.
8. Document why this would be the most effective solution:
   a. Gather supporting evidence from authorities that reinforces your point of view.
   b. Anticipate other points of view, other proposed solutions. Demonstrate why these would not be as effective as yours. Again cite authorities.
9. Relate the audience to the proposed solution; why they should support it:
   a. State that a solution can only come about through their active support.
   b. Ask if they want to suffer the consequences outlined in paragraph 5 above. If not, then they have no choice but to cooperate.
10. A call to action; how they can support it:
    a. Give them a program of action.
11. Conclusion. The result of their action:

a. Sketch out the beneficial changes that would result from their taking the prompt and vigorous action you recommend. Benefits to:
  (1) Themselves personally.
  (2) Their children.
  (3) Society as a whole and a better, more wholesome way of life for all.

You will notice that there are a number of advantages to constructing a detailed working outline such as this one. The speech breaks itself up into clearly defined and manageable sections. You know at all times where you are going, what points you are leading up to. In addition, if there are any holes in your research the outline reveals them. This helps you focus on what further background material you need to bolster your thesis. A word of warning here. It is entirely possible that the evidence you turn up will not support your premise. You may not find the quotes you want, and authorities may differ with you on the analysis of the problem. In that case, you would be wise to rethink your assumptions and perhaps moderate your views. However, a man who agrees to deliver a speech on television violence and its effects on the young probably harbors strong feelings on the subject.

You will also notice that the outline is general rather than specific. There is no mention, for example, of what the recommended program of action should be. This is deliberate. Remember, we are dealing with the most effective way of arranging the key elements of a speech so that a basic proposition is proved and an audience moved.

It may sound cynical, but I could put together an equally forceful outline on the thesis: "The Dangers of Violence on Television Are Overrated." I'm talking about an *outline* now —the blueprint or general plan of the speech, and not the speech itself. Frankly, I doubt if I could write such a speech effectively because my personal convictions run the other way. But there is no question that I could play the devil's advocate and organize what would be the most effective way of proving the other point of view, even if I couldn't do a good job of writing it.

Review Your Outline

An outline, once it has been committed to paper, is not a sacred document. It can easily be full of false assumptions and misleading implications. It may even be totally unworkable. Your final act, before you write, should be to review your entire outline, step by step. Check each statement. Can it be verified? Look at each conclusion you make. Can every one be supported by facts? Do your thoughts flow in an orderly fashion with each section building on the previous one? Have you left out anything? Can you add anything? It is essential that you establish satisfactory answers to all of these questions because the detailed outline you have prepared is your working document. It is the blueprint of your speech. An architect, when he draws blueprints for the house he is to build, makes sure that everything is in its proper place.

A friend of mine, who is an architect, told me about the first residence he ever designed. It was a classroom exercise, but even so he put a great deal of ingenuity and imagination into the project. His professor quite properly congratulated him on his effort, but gave him a failing grade for the assignment. It turned out that he had forgotten to put a door in the wall of the master bedroom. If the house had been built according to his plans, there was no way anyone could get into that room.

It took the review of an objective outsider to discover the flaw. Unfortunately, when most of us review our own freshly completed work we are often not as objective as we should be. An effective solution is to put the work aside for several days. Don't look at it, and try to forget about it. Then, after a period of separation, bring it out and review your outline as dispassionately as you can. You'll be surprised at how many worthwhile changes you can make. And besides, this advice gives you a handy excuse for putting off the writing process for a few more days.

Summary and Checklist

After you've selected your topic (or had it assigned to you) and well before you actually start to write, run over this checklist and see if you have satisfactory answers to all these questions.

1. *Approach.* Have you settled on an approach to your subject matter? Will you be going into your subject deeply, or are you just going to hit the high spots? Is your approach attuned to the audience you will be facing?

2. *Thesis.* What is your principal thesis? Write it down in fifty words or less. If it needs more words, then your central thesis is probably too diffuse. Think it through again. Your message has got to be sharp, clear, and simple—especially to yourself.

3. *Theme.* What is your attitude toward your own thesis? How will you present it to your audience? Do you know now what the general tone of your speech is going to be?

4. *Random Notes.* Have you made a collection of notes on your subject? Do they begin to point in the direction of an outline, and do they give you an idea of the kind of research you will have to do in order to support your thesis and theme?

5. *Research.* Are you just collecting facts, or is your research moving in a productive fashion?

6. *Where To Look.* In addition to newspaper and magazine clippings that you have gathered yourself, have you consulted:

a. Your librarian
b. Encyclopedias
c. The *Reader's Guide to Periodical Literature*
d. Almanacs
e. The *New York Times Index*
f. Trade associations
g. Government publications
h. Experts in your subject matter

7. *Initial Outline.* Have you constructed a preliminary outline that provides you with a rough idea of how the speech will hang together?

8. *Working Outline.* Is your working outline complete and comprehensive? Does it show you in detail exactly where you are going?

9. *Review.* Have you reviewed your working outline carefully? Is every point in its proper place? Does it make sense? Are your conclusions warranted? Are they sound? Are they convincing?

If your answer is yes to all of these questions, you will have prepared a firm foundation for the writing process to follow. There are no more excuses for you to delay any longer. Still, if you are ingenious enough, I'm sure you can think of a few good reasons to keep from getting to work.

CHAPTER 3

Sitting Down to Write

Eventually, though, your excuses will run out. No more re-search is possible. You will have run to earth every scrap of information of any conceivable value. You will have gath-ered the quotes you intend to use and the authorities you expect to cite. Your outline is solidly constructed and highly detailed and it rings entirely true at every point. It seems as though you have everything at your fingertips. But even so, as you write there are a number of general principles you should bear in mind, and a couple of tricks of the trade that might prove useful.

Grammar

Quite a few people are concerned with grammatical con-struction, and it is true the rules of English grammar are many and bewildering. Never forget, however, that you are writing a composition that is not meant to be read. It's meant to be listened to. With the exception of my fourth grade teacher, I have never encountered anyone who worries about grammar when he speaks his native language. For most of us, conversation comes naturally and easily. Generally, we express ourselves with strong colloquial speech and don't fret needlessly about obeying a set of rules that we've forgotten, if we ever bothered to learn them in the first place.

There is a story told about a speech Winston Churchill once wrote when he occupied one of his many ministerial posts in the British government. Governments being what they are, Churchill had to submit his talk to various departments for comment and approval. One overzealous critic came down quite heavily on the Churchill prose, altering a number of sentences because they ended with a preposition. For some reason I have never fully grasped, it is considered poor form to say, "Who does he work for?" What they want you to say instead is, "For whom does he work?" I take exception to this sort of nit picking, and apparently, so did Churchill. When he saw how the rhythm of his sentences had been destroyed by the grammarian in his department, an outraged Churchill crossed out all the objections and scrawled in the margin, "This is the kind of nonsense up with which I will not put."

The best rule on the question of employing proper grammatical construction in a speech is this: if it sounds right to the ear, then that's the way to say it. And remember, a preposition is just fine to end a sentence with.

Your Speech Consists of Words

Although this may sound like the most banal observation you have ever encountered, let's consider it for a moment. Words are the way to express your ideas, and the selection of the most effective words to get across your thoughts is a difficult and complex business. Because it is a living language, English is constantly changing. Certain word usages have become obsolete and new ones are developing. Some words have been overused and whatever punch they might have had at one time has been dissipated. So choose your words carefully for their strength, for their shade of meaning, and above all for their graphic, vivid qualities.

ACTIVE WORDS

We have all suffered through articles that are stale, uninspired, and dull. And yet the same subject, in the hands of another writer, can come alive and rivet our attention. It's true that the good writer has a knack for presenting his material in an interesting fashion. He knows how to tell a good story—even if it is nonfiction. But in addition he's developed the ability to choose active words that fairly jump out at you from the page. "My fellow citizens, I would appreciate your attention for a few moments," is not quite as effective as, "Friends, Romans, countrymen, lend me your ears."

Here are a few more examples. A speaker at a school board meeting urging the construction of a new gym could say: "The facility is essential to the physical development of the young people of our community." Or he could put it this way: "A new gym is going to mean stronger kids and a stronger community." There's nothing dramatic about the difference between the two. But the second is much cleaner and more direct because it does away with words and phrases like "facility" and "the physical development" which are not active or alive.

An argument against closing a branch library in the community could be phrased like this: "Withdrawing these services will deprive our citizens of a needed opportunity for cultural enrichment." Or it could be done this way: "Putting a padlock on the library is like putting a padlock on our minds."

A man and his wife return from a trip to Mexico City, and he describes their experiences to fellow members of his church group: "The altitude of Mexico City is high enough to cause a breathing problem." That's a dead statement. But it could come alive for his audience if he said, "The air is so thin up there, a man can get out of breath just by lying down."

THE VIVID VERB

The right verb can pump new life into a tired sentence. Even more, it can convey a graphic image of what you are trying to say. "He swam through the water" describes a certain event. You know that the writer is referring to a person who moved through the water from point *A* to point *B*. But if he "churned," "knifed," or "paddled" through the water, you know a great deal more about what happened and the scene begins to take on some color.

Learning to use more interesting verbs is largely a matter of habit. People fall back on the same old familiar words because they've never taken the trouble to experiment. As an exercise, the next time you read an article pay particular attention to the verbs. Make a mental note on how many you can change. You'll see that often you will have changed the entire meaning of the sentence. "The man marched down the street," gives an entirely different mental impression than, "The man staggered down the street." And yet we've only changed the verb. And now compare both of these with, "The man moved down the street." This sentence describes the event. Whether he "marched" or "staggered," he still "moved." But it's not vivid enough. It doesn't convey as much information as either of the more descriptive verbs.

THE DEAD PHRASE

Most speeches are full of dead phrases. People seem to expect them and speakers seldom disappoint them. "Ladies and gentlemen, it is an honor and a very great privilege to be with you this evening," is one of the deadest I know. It is also one of the most useful, as we shall see later.

"In order to support my statement, I will ask your permission to quote some interesting statistics." That is one of my favorite dead phrases. What in the world is wrong with, "Here are some facts that back me up."

"Now, I would like to cover the following points in a certain way that will seem puzzling at first. However, as I go through them, I think you will agree they make sense." I will never agree that the speaker can possibly make sense on any subject if he insists on talking to me in this fashion.

Dead phrases simply take up time. They do not advance the argument. They are not entertaining. They perform no function whatsoever. Speakers use them largely as a crutch to get from one point to another. Look at every sentence you write. Does it contribute to what you are trying to say? Or are you just letting out a little meaningless gas? Take care to do away with any deadwood in your talk. If I happen to be in the audience when you deliver it, I'll cheer loudly.

Common Word Traps

Familiarity breeds carelessness, and this is especially true of the way we use words. I'm not talking about the more correctable faults of writing a dull word or dead phrase. I mean the small ruts our everyday speech settles into if we don't check ourselves.

THE TIRED CLICHÉ

We all know the more common clichés—stubborn as a mule, sly as a fox, high as a kite—and I think most of us have the sense to avoid them. But there is still another kind of cliché that so often creeps into a speech and that is somehow characteristic of speeches more than of any other form of communication.

When I hear the speaker tell his audience that they can take "justifiable pride in the accomplishments of the medical profession," I wonder if I will ever be privileged to hear a man say that it is possible to take "unjustifiable pride" in whatever it is he's talking about. How many times have you heard that phrase in a speech? Unless you take care, you will likely use it yourself.

"Of course, there remains much to be done, but I am confident we can achieve our goal with your support." With slight variations, this probably ranks as the most overused phrase in the entire repertoire of dull clichés. And there are dozens more like them. Be on the lookout. If the sentence sounds peculiarly like others you have heard time and time again, try saying it another way.

REDUNDANCIES AND OTHER IRRELEVANCIES

These find their way into a speech so easily because the writer is simply not sufficiently critical of his own work or precise with his own words. How simple it is to write, "And now I want to discuss the following events in chronological order, as they occurred."

Another one I rather like came in a political speech when the candidate was saying about his opponent, "Even though he is occasionally effective, he is seldom so."

Still another expression that appears in speeches with surprising regularity is the "What-did-he-say?" phrase. This is a sort of verbal double take that may sound all right, but doesn't really make any sense.

"It was a long road, but very narrow," is one I'm fond of. But I think my all-time favorite is, "The large group of people included a horse." Finally, I read this one in a speech: "The small, neighborhood retail merchant can make a good living before he goes broke." Eventually, I understood what the writer was driving at. He meant that, even though the merchant operated a successful business, he had to guard himself constantly against a number of factors in order to keep from bankruptcy.

These may be amusing—but only when they happen to other speakers. About the only man I know who has ever profited from language like that is Casey Stengel. But I suppose if you're a banker, it's all right.

THE BIG WORD

I have worked with many speakers over the years and I have found, generally, that those who are new at the game are very conscious of their dignity. They are partial to the ponderous word, choosing it every time over the simpler, more direct one. For some reason they believe the audience will be more impressed if they clothe their thoughts with measured, weighty phrases. They simply refuse to believe that what the audience appreciates is a direct, easy to understand approach.

"The consistent underachievers in the school exhibited the most acute antisocial behavioral patterns," really means, "The youngsters who always did poorly at school showed a great deal of hostility."

JARGON, PROFESSIONAL AND OTHERWISE

This leads directly into one of my pet peeves with many speakers—their fondness for the jargon of their profession. If a man uses the words "underachievers" and "antisocial behavioral patterns," I'll bet a dollar he is either an educator, a sociologist, or a psychologist. If he's none of these, then he's just pretentious.

The most common offenders are members of the scientific

establishment with their references to "on time, real time operations," and bureaucrats from the government who can't seem to talk in any other fashion. But you can, so stay away from jargon. It's bad for you image-wise.

The Opening

The opening of any speech is certainly the most difficult part to deliver and, for me at any rate, the most difficult part to write. The delivery problem stems from the fact that a speaker is usually at his most nervous when he begins his talk. Later on he relaxes. But the first few seconds on his feet can be a rocky time for even the experienced lecturer. And that is one reason why so many speeches begin with a dead phrase. Unless you're absolutely paralyzed by stage fright, even the most nervous beginner can usually get through the sentence, "Ladies and gentlemen, it is indeed a pleasure and an honor to be with you this evening," without too much thought or effort.

Then, too, the opening is the time when the speaker must establish his relationship with his audience. People sitting in a hall have a tendency to make snap judgments about the man on the platform, and they usually make them within the first minute. First impressions count.

In addition, the opening of a speech presents hazards for the other side of the platform. The speaker is introduced, and the audience settles down to hear what he is going to say. And I mean settles down. So often at the beginning of a talk you hear chairs creaking, coughs erupting from all over the house, and the scrape of feet on the floor. The audience is quite literally getting itself arranged comfortably so that it can give the speaker its attention for the next twenty minutes or so. Under these circumstances, it's a little unfair if the speaker drops his big bombshell at the outset. A speaker who sets out to warn his audience of approaching urban blight would not be well-advised to start with, "The city we're in this evening will be a deserted graveyard of empty buildings within twenty years." He's almost certain to get a buzz of "What was that he said?" from the many listeners who weren't quite sure they had heard him.

So work into your main thesis. Don't start right off with it. Open with a dead phrase. It's easier on you and protocol usually requires it. Then do one of two things. Either relate yourself to the subject matter of your speech or relate yourself to your audience.

By relating yourself to your subject matter, I mean this. In a talk on philately, you might say, "I know every speaker always tells his audience how delighted he is to be with them, but in my case the feeling is genuine. I have been collecting stamps for nearly forty years, and I've never lost my enthusiasm. I can talk for hours on the subject, but I promise you I won't." This has the advantage of giving your audience an insight of how you stand with respect to your subject matter. And by casually dropping the impressive figure of forty years, you've convinced them in one sentence that you know what you're talking about. Now, they're ready to hear what you have to say.

Relating yourself to your subject matter can be carried to extremes. I would not advise a speaker on the breeding of German shepherds to start out by saying, "Those who know me best tell me that it's absolutely right for me to be here to talk about dogs because I'm such a son of a bitch."

Relating yourself to your audience is usually a very effective device. You somehow become one of them, or, if not, at least an admirer. "I have always admired the aims of the Rotary Clubs, and I haven't met a Rotarian I didn't like. The one regret I've had is that I've never lived in one place long enough to join the local Rotary. I'm sure you fellows would make me welcome. But I'd know I couldn't commit myself to the long-term kind of community service you do, and so my conscience wouldn't let me join." Start a talk to a Rotary group with those words, and I'll guarantee you'll have them on your side, if you don't lose them by being long-winded.

Get to the Point

The kind of opening we've been talking about should not be more than two or three paragraphs at the most. Flattery is well-received, and it's good to know where you stand in relationship to your subject, but there comes a time in too many speeches when the audience feels like shouting, "For heaven's sake man, get to the point." After all, the people out front have come to hear you tell them something. They could just as easily have gone to the movies or stayed home and watched television. The speaker who begins with a pleasantry and follows it with a good anecdote will have the audience in the palm of his hand. But if he tacks on one funny story after the other, the laughter will soon die and he will be met, before too many minutes, with a roomful of impatient stares.

Start the ball rolling early in the game. If you haven't begun to work on your thesis by the middle of the first page of your speech, throw it away and start all over. But that is easier said than done. How do you get into your subject in a way that grabs your audience's attention? There are dozens of ways, of course, but there is one that I recommend as a surefire formula. If you possibly can, do it by means of an anecdote. Let's go back to our example of the speech on television violence, and let's assume you managed to find an anecdote that was specific and full of human interest. You might lead into your main point like this:

"Michael Blake was a normal, happy, eight-year-old. Or so it appeared. Michael lived with his mother and father and his five-year-old sister, Patty, in Bethesda, Maryland. He did what any other eight-year-old did—he went to school, rode his bike, played baseball, and watched television for about four hours each day. Neither of his parents paid any attention to what he watched—until one day Michael's mother heard a scream from the living room. She rushed in to find Patty lying on the floor, bleeding heavily from a scalp wound. Michael had smashed her over the head with a folding bridge chair. Patty suffered a slight concussion and needed eight stitches to close up her wound. Michael said later he did it because she was teasing him and he wanted her to stop. Besides, he didn't think it would hurt her. People hit each other all the time in the cartoons he watched on television, and they didn't bleed."

That's a pretty effective opening for your thesis, and I admit such neat anecdotes are hard to come by. But they don't have to be that dramatic to be telling. Your speech on stamps could begin by remembering the first foreign stamp you ever saw and how it made geography come alive for you.

Or, if you're telling a group about recent advances in petroleum technology, forget about the technological side at first and reduce it to human terms. Give them an imaginary anecdote about the various everyday, routine things that you or your wife did that morning, and show how each is related, in some way, to your subject matter.

If no anecdotes are available, make one up. I know that sounds as if I'm contradicting my earlier admonition that a speech is not a work of fiction. But just as there is poetic license, so there is a certain license allowed in speech making. However, the anecdote should be based on fact. If it didn't actually happen, it should have. Besides, if you're still uneasy about misrepresentation, let your audience in on the truth.

"Of course, what I've told you never really happened. But the important point is that it could have happened . . . and just the way I described it to you, because of the amazing advances made by modern petroleum technology." A simple statement like that gets you off the hook and you will have made your point.

Later, as you become more experienced, you will not need to rely exclusively on the anecdotal form to get to the first point of your speech. But even so, I can think of nothing that does the job better, or no device that is easier to use. Far more difficult is the problem of getting off your first point and moving on to the next one.

The Transition

When you've made the outline for your speech, you will notice that it is a listing, set down in logical order, of the various principal points you will be discussing. When you're writing about one of these points, you may be quite eloquent. But there comes a time when you have to wrap things up and move along to the next section. The process is called writing a transitional paragraph. Many writers find this awkward and difficult to do. And yet a good speech should be written in such a way that it seems to flow effortlessly from point to point. The seams of the speech should be stitched into place so skillfully that they don't show. This naturally presents problems.

It is too often solved by means of phrases like, "Now, let's move on to the next point," or, "Putting aside these observations for a moment, let me draw your attention to. . . ." When you fall back on these, you sound like a man giving the audience a guided tour through his own ideas. They're looking at your ideas, but they're not participating in them.

The best way to get through a transitional paragraph gracefully is to think about it well before you get there. Don't paint yourself into a verbal corner where you can't get out without making messy tracks all over the floor.

Let's assume you're talking to a group about the develop-

ment of photography. Your outline for the section you're
about to write reads like this:

a. The disadvantages of the *camera obscura.*
b. The development of the lens and the shutter.

You wind up *a* with a sentence that reads, "Remarkable as
the invention was, its weakest point was the very feature that
made it work—the tiny hole that admitted the light."

Now, your problem is how to get from *a* to *b*. What is the
smoothest way to work into a discussion of the application of
the lens to the development of the camera?

A start like, "They were grinding lenses in northern Eu-
rope in the sixteenth century," is simply too abrupt. Read the
two phrases together and you'll see that the gears are being
shifted too rapidly.

On the other hand, "Forgetting about the *camera obscura*
for a moment, let us go back several hundred years in time,"
is a guided tour phrase.

But how about this: "It soon became evident that the hole
had to be fitted with some sort of device to control the
amount of light gathered by the camera. Fortunately, an op-
tical instrument that gathered and focused light had been
invented many years earlier. This simple device was known
as a lens."

The key is to take a trigger word from the previous sentence or thought and incorporate it into the next one. The
first thought ends with the phrase "the tiny hole that admitted the light." The next sentence repeats the word "hole"
and introduces the concept of gathering light. This concept,
in turn, is used in the third sentence to introduce the lens,
which is the subject of the next principal section to be discussed.

So when you get to the end of one of your principal points
and you find you're stuck, carry over one of your words or

phrases into the following sentence. You'll be surprised at how smooth the transition will sound.

The Tone of Your Speech

The tone of any speech is, to a large measure, determined by the delivery style of the speaker. But not entirely. The words on paper can express anger, exasperation, outrage, hope, or conciliation. Words are extremely powerful instruments, and great care should be taken in their use. The wrong or over-stated phrase that looks perfectly innocent on paper can give quite the opposite impression when spoken out loud.

On the issue of the closing of a branch library in the community, these words might appear to be appropriate: "Really, the choice is quite simple—either you are in favor of the intellectual development of this community or you're not." Unfortunately, however, a statement like that can easily get any audience's back up. The issue is not as simple as that. There are other considerations. Perhaps the money can be used to better advantage in meeting some other community need. Your position is too harsh, too uncompromising.

WORDS CAN CHANGE

Watch your language carefully at all times. Words may have one meaning to you and an entirely different meaning to someone else. The word "liberal," for example, was once held in esteem by everyone who was not of a "conservative" persuasion. Now, of course, both members of the John Birch Society and the radical left find common ground in their disdain for a "liberal"—for quite different reasons it is true.

SPEAK SOFTLY

You may feel strongly about a subject, and, as a speaker, it is your responsibility to communicate your feelings to your audience and persuade them that you are correct. But don't bully them. They will resent it. Show them the light; don't blind them with it. The most effective speakers present their arguments in such a way that their audience is convinced that they have found out the truth by themselves. Read Marc Anthony's funeral oration in Shakespeare's *Julius Caesar.* The speech is a masterful example of how to manipulate a crowd into accepting a particular point of view without beating them over the head with it.

CHANGE YOUR PACE

If you speak for twenty minutes in the same style, the effect will be monotonous. Vary the length of your sentences. Wake your audience up with an occasional question: "Do we really want this to happen in our community?" In baseball, one of the most effective pitches is the change of pace. Try to develop a similar delivery when you speak in public.

HUMOR

The ability to tell a good story is a rare quality. It may be easy to find one that exactly illustrates the point you are trying to make, but not many people can tell it. I once wrote a speech for the chief financial executive of a large oil company, who had many fine qualities. Humor, however, was not one of them. As we were discussing his speech, I could tell something was bothering him. Finally, as I rose to leave, he came out with it. "You know," he said, "I've never had anyone write a speech for me before." I assured him it was going to be far less painful than going to the dentist. "Yes," he said anxiously, "I'm sure it's going to be all right. But do me a favor. Don't put any jokes in it. You see, I'm not a very funny man." Here was a speaker who knew his own limitations. He knew that many after-dinner speakers laced their talk with wisecracks, and he was painfully aware that he wasn't up to delivering them. Needless to say, I wrote a very sober speech. And he was surprisingly effective, because it suited his personality. Don't strain for humor. If you can do it easily and well, your audience will appreciate it. If you're awkward and unsure of yourself, the result will be embarrassment for all concerned.

Get Involved

I have said before that a speech is not a cold recitation of certain facts. The audience has come to hear you as well as your subject matter. Don't stay aloof from them or you will lose them.

THE PASSIVE VOICE

All too frequently we hear in speeches phrases like, "It has been observed that exercise, regularly taken, improves an individual's sense of well-being." What individuals are we talking about, and who has done the observing? Put your arms around the statement and make it more relevant to your audience. It is much more powerful to say, "You and I both know we feel better when we exercise." Instead of "It can be stated with some justification . . ." a better phrase would be, "Yes, I admit there is some justification. . . ." Don't be afraid to involve yourself and your audience in the subject you're discussing.

THE OUTSIDE AUTHORITY

Many speakers don't try to prove their points. They rely on an outside authority to do it for them. They make a few statements that invite a conclusion and then turn to a quotation, which they introduce with a phrase such as, "I think we can all agree with Winston Churchill when he said . . . ." Now Winston Churchill is an impressive figure, no doubt about it. But it so happens that the audience has come to hear the speaker and not Winston Churchill. Quotes are all right used sparingly. Unquestionably they lend authority to what you are trying to prove. But don't make the mistake of including too many quotations in your talk. They do not take the place of original thought.

Still another crutch is the habit of quoting excessively from various publications. "The January bulletin of the American Management Association had some interesting observations on this problem," is all right if the observations are short. But I have heard talks where well over half the time was given to quotations from magazines and trade publications. Children may enjoy being read to, but an audience of adults will find it unenlightening. Say it in your own words.

STATISTICS

The inexperienced speaker is very partial to statistics. He seems to feel that if he's got the numbers to back him up, then he's made his point. What he forgets is that numbers and statistics are only as effective as their interpretation. Besides, an audience simply cannot absorb a long recitation of figures. Repeat this phrase to someone, and do it only once. "In 1963, unemployment figures in the industry rose 4.3 percent. In 1964 they were down 1.2 percent. Then in 1965,

1966, and 1967 they showed a steady increase that totaled a full 7.6 percent above comparable figures five years earlier." Now ask your friend what happened to the unemployment figures in 1964. Go easy on statistics. But when you *do* use them, make sure you explain what they mean. Most figures are really dead until you measure their consequences in such a way that they have an impact on your audience.

The Climax

Good suspense movies always have their climactic scene. So do good speeches. The climax of a speech is what should stay with an audience long after it has forgotten your initial thesis. Unfortunately, too many speeches return in the end to their original statement. For example, in the speech whose thesis is: "Violence on Television Gives Children a Distorted View of Life," it would be a mistake to start out with this assumption, prove it thoroughly to your audience, and then end with the lame statement, "And so you see, violence does indeed give children a distorted view of life." Your audience will be dissatisfied with this, and rightfully so. Their feeling will be, "All right, you've shown us, but so what? What do we do about it."

In this particular case, the climax should be a presentation of how all concerned persons can band together to prevent the situation from continuing. It's the "Here's how you can begin right now to enjoy the rewards that come from the fascinating hobby of stamp collecting." In another context, it's the "This is what we can all do to save the library," or "Look around you. Now that you've got an insight, see the number of ways petroleum technology affects you each day."

A good, rousing climax is never tacked on to the end of a speech as an afterthought. Know what your climax is going to be right from the beginning and work up to it. It is the target, the goal of your speech, and everything that precedes it should contribute to its strength.

The Ending

The ending of a speech is often as difficult to write as the beginning. You can't very well fashion a ringing climax and then sit down abruptly. However, the formula for an effective ending is not difficult. It is simply an extension of the climax, a statement of how the action you have urged will affect the well-being of your audience or the course of history, depending upon how ambitious your speech has been.

Here is an example of a typical ending. Immediately after the action-oriented climax comes the final sentence: "And if we fully understand the problem and take the trouble to do something about it, I think you will find your own lives a little richer and our town a more pleasant place to live in. Thank you." Over and out. Simple and direct. It merely points out the consequences of a certain line of action in a general and unspecific fashion. There is an unmistakable note of finality to it that rounds out whatever you have said previously.

Invite Criticism

A man is supposed to be his own poorest critic. But I happen to disagree with that. I think it is possible for a writer to judge his work in a reasonably objective manner. At the same time, it can be extremely useful to expose your speech to an outside evaluation. After all, you're going to have to unveil it publicly anyway, so why not limit your risks? But remember that every man has his own approach to whatever problem you're writing about. If your critic says he doesn't understand what you mean in one section, or if he tells you that he doesn't agree with your conclusions, you would be well-advised to listen to him carefully. If he doesn't understand you, then perhaps you can express yourself more clearly. If he doesn't agree with one of your major points, hear him out. He may have some information that you've overlooked.

However, if he takes objection to your language, or suggests that you say something in a slightly different way, I wouldn't pay too much attention. That is perhaps the way he would say it, but then he's not giving the speech. You are. It must be written in a style that suits your particular way of speaking. It all boils down to this: if the criticism touches on content, pay attention to it. If it relates to style, you and you alone must be the final judge.

Summary and Checklist

Writing in a style that is natural and easy is perhaps the most helpful advice anyone can give. But as you approach the task of composition, bear in mind the following checklist.

1. *Grammar.* Don't overly concern yourself with it. If it sounds right when you say it out loud, then it is right.

2. *Words.* Take a little trouble to find the most descriptive word, the colorful phrase. Don't be a lazy writer. Avoid the humdrum and the too familiar.

a. *Active words:* Is there a more interesting and graphic way to express yourself? Experiment. Have a little fun.

b. *The vivid verb:* Search for the most descriptive verb. Practice using different verbs.

c. *The dead phrase:* Guard against sentences that do nothing to advance your thesis. Eliminate dead patches in your prose.

3. *Common Word Traps.* Too many speeches fall into ruts. Break some fresh ground.

a. *The tired cliché:* Avoid the familiar, the well-worn phrase. Your audience will be grateful.

b. *Redundancies:* Keep a sharp lookout for them. They creep in because you allow yourself to become careless. And while you're about it, don't open yourself to ridicule with a meaningless phrase.

c. *The big word:* Always use the simple word. You don't "employ" a hammer. You "use" it.

d. *Jargon:* A sure way to puzzle and alienate your audience.

4. *The Opening.* Start out with an anecdote (make one up if you have to) that does one of two things. It relates you either to your subject or to your audience.

5. *Get to the Point.* Move right into your subject. You should be well on the way toward developing your thesis before the end of the first page.

6. *The Transition.* Getting from one point to another can present difficulties. Use the "chain" method, linking key words or phrases from one sentence to the next.

7. *Your Tone.* Words are tricky and can convey the wrong impression. Make sure that your tone is exactly right.

8. *Get Involved.* Don't remove yourself from your subject. Your audience has come to hear you. Watch out for:

a. *The passive voice:* Avoid phrases like "It is understood," and use instead, "I understand."

b. *The outside authority:* Quote him sparingly.

c. *Statistics:* Figures themselves prove nothing. Interpret their meaning whenever you use them.

9. *The Climax.* Don't simply repeat your thesis. A climax is a call to action.

10. *The Ending.* Don't just suddenly stop. Round your speech out with an ending that has a note of finality.

11. *Invite Criticism.* But distinguish between criticism of form and content. Accept comments on content. You be the final judge on style.

CHAPTER 4

Speeches for Most Occasions

Most speeches—I'd say well over ninety percent of them—can be classified into four broad categories. I'm not talking about the "heavyweight" speech that gets reported in the press. When a prominent business executive is asked to give his views on the subject of east-west trade, he turns the assignment over to a professional speech writer whose job it is to come up with interesting and provocative observations, together with solutions that hold promise. Beyond these, there are the thousands upon thousands of "grass-roots" speeches that businessmen and community leaders are constantly being asked to prepare and deliver to local organizations. Since these are the ones you will most likely give, this chapter will deal with the more common occasions and audiences you will face in your career as a speaker.

Your Occupation

Without question, most speakers address themselves to one aspect or another of their everyday working lives. A man's job is what he knows best, and so it should come as no surprise that he is frequently asked to speak about it in public. And his job doesn't have to be particularly exotic or glamorous for the requests to pour in. People are naturally interested in how other people live. The subject of what goes on behind the scenes of a large supermarket can be a fascinating one, and the manager of such an operation can easily hold an audience's attention by a discussion of his activities and how they affect the shopping public.

However, the most common occasion for a speaker is when he is asked to address a meeting, a luncheon, or a convention of his fellows. This is in the case of a member of the traffic department of a manufacturing firm talking to representatives of the trucking industry, or a financial executive talking to a group of accountants. Because his audience is so knowledgeable about the subject, the speaker must be careful to keep his remarks relevant and very much to the point.

A BUSINESS OCCASION

Usually, when you are asked to speak before a business or professional group, the organizing committee will suggest a topic. In most cases, you should be able to talk about it easily and well because, after all, you have been handpicked for the assignment. But if, for any reason, the subject does not suit you, or you think that another related area would be more fruitful, don't hesitate to tell the committee. Since the speech is ultimately your responsibility, you should have a certain freedom of choice. Don't let them bully you. But, on the other hand, do them the courtesy of registering your objection and suggesting an alternative early in the game so they can proceed with drawing up the rest of the program. Once your topic has been selected, consult freely with a member of the program committee. Solicit his advice about your approach and, if you're not familiar with the particular group you're scheduled to address, ask him about their specific interests. A few simple inquiries will help you focus your ideas and, before long, some concrete ideas will emerge.

However, before you proceed with them, get the advice of your new-found contact. Try them out on him and see if he thinks they're appropriate for the audience or the occasion. You will find his help freely given and extremely useful. To cite an example, you might elect to talk on the subject of "Quotas for Imported Steel" before a group of specialty steel distributors, only to find, after you've finished, that they'd heard a speech on the very same subject the last time they met. A few well-chosen questions soon after you've accepted your engagement will save you from walking into situations like that.

In preparing for speeches before those who are engaged in your own line of work or some activity related to it, here are a few basic rules to remember:

1. Avoid generalities. Your audience is informed, aware, and interested. They don't need polite phrases, and they don't want to be talked down to. You should have some ideas and convictions to share with them. After all, you're all in the same or closely allied business.

2. Make a list of the five or six most important or controversial questions facing your industry.

3. Make a similar list of the innovations or developments that would, in your opinion, most benefit your industry. Keep these as succinct as you can. A sentence or two for each, at the most.

4. Study these two lists and ask yourself which entries appeal to you. Soon you will have a tentative list of subjects.

5. Take the controversial questions you have chosen. Can you come up with meaningful and interesting solutions? Are they workable? Make sure that you are not repeating well-worn answers. You should make a novel contribution to each issue.

6. What about desirable innovations or developments? Stretch your mind and let your imagination flow. Are these realistic? What would their consequence be? How would your job and the jobs of your listeners be made more interesting and rewarding if they came about?

7. By being very rigorous in your self-questioning, you will by now have discarded a number of early possibilities, and you will be left with perhaps three or four topics which seem promising and which you are qualified to talk about.

8. Perhaps, at this point, there is no question in your own mind. You know exactly what you want to talk about. Fine. But if the three or four possibilities all look equally attractive, and you can't decide which one to choose, ask the representative of the group you're going to address. He'll probably have an instinct for the right topic. If not, then talk it over at the office. Some outside views are very helpful at this point, so don't hesitate to listen. But don't let anyone tell you what conclusions to reach and, above all, don't accept advice on how to construct your speech. That's your responsibility. All you want now is a general reaction to a topic. Would anyone be interested in hearing a discussion of that subject?

9. Once you've made your selection, begin the process outlined in Chapter 2. Make your random notes and proceed from there to a detailed outline.

In the speaking situation we're talking about now, your two key considerations should be controversial issues and new developments. A controversial issue could be legislation that might affect your industry, or the danger of imports, or the need to develop entirely new work practices. A discussion of innovations could center on new products, or new applica-

tions for existing products. You could focus on a trend you've
noticed within your own industry that might have powerful
effects on your audience. In any event, if you take either of
these two concepts as your starting point, you will have
taken out a guarantee that your subject matter will be of interest to your listeners.

A CHURCH OR SOCIAL GROUP

Burning issues are not really appropriate here. Even if you
do manage to rouse the group with some new development
that may affect your occupation, they're not going to be able
to do anything about it. They may have an interest in what
you do, but they hardly share your concern. A most helpful
approach, when you're to address a group like this, would be
to examine where their lives touch your business or profession.

This is relatively easy if your days are spent dealing directly with the public. If you happen to be a retail merchant,
or if you're in any one of the service industries, your relationship with the public is crucial to your success. And so it
might even benefit you professionally if you were to use that
relationship as the point of attack for organizing your
speech. What about these as topics:

1. *The Customer Is Always Right—Most of the Time.*
This could be a plea, on your part, for a greater understanding by the public of some of your problems. Your point is
that you do really try very hard to provide service, but that
occasionally the unreasonable attitude of a customer makes
it difficult.

2. *Behind the Sale.* All that most customers see is the mer-
chandise on the shelf (or the immediate availability of the
service). Describe the enormous effort that goes into providing the convenience they have come to expect. They might
appreciate your service a little more if they knew.

3. *Knowing What You Want.* A retailer who does not supply the public with what it wants will soon go out of business. Talk to your audience about the sometimes tricky process of keeping up with the public's fast-changing tastes. Here's a side of your business they've probably never even thought of.

These three random examples have a single factor in common. They discuss one aspect of the relationship between your business and the audience. With a little thought, you will be able to develop others much better suited to your own particular line of work.

Such an approach does not seem quite as easy if you happen to be, say, a cost accountant or a government employee. But the general principle still applies. What is there about your work that would interest your audience? I am not suggesting that you provide your listeners with a detailed job description. That's of interest only to your personnel department. Rather, try to find the human side of your activities and relate that to your listeners.

If you really are a cost accountant, for example, you could show the value of your function by applying cost accounting principles to the running of a family. Everyone sitting in front of you is a member of a family, and many of them have the responsibility of managing it. And the problem of where the money goes is a universal one. Invent an imaginary family and catalog some of its problems because of a careless approach to expenditures. Then show how the discipline of your profession would set to work to solve these problems. From there, it is a relatively simple step to pointing out how larger business enterprises employ your skills and why they consider them essential.

But don't get too detailed. Confine your observations and description to the general rather than to the specific. A group like this will get more out of your talk if you leave them with a general impression of what you do.

A SERVICE ORGANIZATION

The Lions, Kiwanis, Rotary Clubs, Elks, and Shriners are a few of the more prominent organizations that attract members who want to combine relaxation with an obligation they feel to community service. The men who join are usually leaders who are interested in getting a real understanding of their own communities. As I suggested earlier, the key to speaking to clubs of this nature is service.

Try to describe how your occupation benefits the community. If your business is part of a chain or a franchise operation, show that the community concern extends from coast to coast. Virtually every national company these days has a well-organized community relations department that stands ready to supply its affiliated businessmen with sufficient literature and background material to make an effective presentation.

To take things a step further, instead of merely describing the services your business renders to the community, you can suggest ways in which you and your audience can work together to make your town or city a better place to live in. However, before you outline any proposal in your speech, it would be wise to consult with a member of the organization in order to get an advance reading of how well your project would be received.

YOUNG PEOPLE

Most young people today are extraordinarily well-informed, and easily bored. Don't try to tell them how important you are or how vital your occupation is. Don't try to persuade them that yours is the career they should follow. They've all decided long ago that they're going to be drummers in a rock band anyway. So they couldn't be less interested.

The emphasis in a talk before a youth group should not be on how something works or why it works. And you certainly shouldn't try to put your occupation into any sort of historical perspective. Instead, look to the future and speculate with them on how the generation they represent will change the way in which you do business.

If this can't be done effectively, you can take a look at what the technology of the future is going to mean to them. If you happen to be a doctor or are connected in any way with health service, for example, talk about how the traditional doctor–patient relationship will be largely obsolete by the time they become adults. They may not be intrigued by advances in medical science, but they might be interested in the application of computers to medicine and how patients will be monitored automatically by electronic equipment and remote terminals.

If you're the manager of a department store, give them a glimpse of how they will do their shopping at a desk-top computer that will place their order and debit their account at the bank all at the same time.

Whatever your trade or occupation, the important point to remember about addressing a gathering of young people is to relate it to the future and not to the present.

Your Interests or Hobbies

People generally put more ingenuity into the pursuit of their leisure time activities than they do into their regular job. They also exhibit so much enthusiasm for their hobby that they are ready to talk about it at length at the slightest invitation. If you also happen to be somewhat of an expert in your outside interest, you will almost certainly be asked to deliver a talk on it.

Unfortunately, however, the very qualities that make the hobbyist such an attractive choice as a speaker are usually the same ones that do him in when he gets up on the platform. He is usually *too* full of his own subject. He is usually *too* enthusiastic about what he's doing. This too often results in a disorganized presentation.

Because it is so hard to be objective about your own enthusiasms, you must exercise self-control when you talk about the subject nearest to your heart. Here is the opening of a speech a dedicated stamp collector could give on his specialty:

"I think that stamp collecting is one of the most interesting and rewarding hobbies a man could have, and tonight I want to tell you why. My interest in stamps goes back to when I was a boy and was given my first stamp catalog. I was fascinated by the doors it opened. I found I could travel anywhere in the world in my imagination, and even today the thrill hasn't left me. Besides the fun, stamp collecting can be a financially rewarding hobby. Why, right now you may have a fortune tucked away in some forgotten box in your own attic and not even know it."

This opening soars right into the subject and bubbles along in a fresh and bright manner. But notice how confusion has already set in. Before the first minute is up, the speaker has presented two quite different theses. Thesis number one is that stamp collecting is great fun, in fact "one of the most interesting and rewarding hobbies a man could have." Thesis number two is that stamp collecting can be a financially rewarding hobby. These two points are not mutually exclusive by any means. But one should be chosen as the main thesis and the other relegated to a secondary position. When you talk about your hobby, whether it is gardening, fly casting, or collecting miniature soldiers, don't let your enthusiasm run away with you. Choose one and only one principal thesis and stick to it. Of course, you can mention other reasons why you find your particular pastime so fascinating or rewarding. But don't give everything equal weight. You will be unable to write a well-organized speech if you do.

Community Affairs

A speech on community affairs is usually a plea for action on some issue that affects nearly every member of your audience. It can relate to your local school, it can be a discussion of real estate tax rates, or it can voice a demand for more recreational facilities for your children. The important point to remember when you give a speech of this type is that your proposal, whatever it is, will almost always affect the pocketbooks of your listeners. You may be on the side of the angels by pointing out the need for improved play areas in your neighborhood. But installing them is going to cost the community, and therefore the people you are talking to, money in the form of an increased tax assessment. So it is essential that you research your facts very carefully. There will always be someone in the audience who is convinced the money can be better spent for some other project. People naturally have different interests and their list of priorities will not be the same as yours. So approach an assignment of this nature with extreme caution, recognizing that you will be facing any one of three different kinds of audience.

A NEUTRAL AUDIENCE

Perhaps the audience you are about to address has no strong feelings on the issues you intend to raise. In that case, you are free to assemble your arguments as forcefully as you are able. Your job will be to get them on your side by the end of your speech, ready and willing to act in the way you advise. You should proceed with developing an outline similar to the one constructed in Chapter 2 for the thesis on television violence. If a neutral audience is still neutral or indifferent at the close of your remarks, you will know that the issue you are so concerned about is not very important to anyone but yourself. Or you could have delivered a hopelessly ineffective speech.

A GENERALLY SYMPATHETIC AUDIENCE

It is reassuring to know, before you mount the platform, that your audience agrees in advance with what you have to say. If you are asked to address a PTA meeting that has been called to protest the lack of school crossing guards at a busy highway intersection, you can be sure they will applaud your righteous indignation at the apparent carelessness of the Board of Education. The temptation, when faced with an audience of this nature, is to go for the grandstand play. If you deliver a ringing denunciation of the system that allows your children to cross the street unprotected, you will be the darling of the crowd. A good rabble-rousing speech may be fun to deliver and even to listen to, but I question whether it has much to do with problem solving. And that really was why the meeting was called in the first place.

When you are dealing with an audience that shares your own personal convictions regarding the issue under discussion, you virtually do away with the process of persuasion. They don't need it. It may be less dramatic, but it is far more helpful to move right in on alternate solutions. Spell out each of the possible answers to your problem and provide a realistic estimate of what each would cost in terms of money or in terms of personal commitment on the part of your listeners. If you sincerely believe one course of action is preferable to all the others, then make that your central thesis and persuade your audience to share your feelings. Tackling the subject in an evenhanded manner such as this immediately signals that you are a leader and a voice worth listening to.

A HOSTILE AUDIENCE

It is an unsettling experience to accept a speaking engagement where you agree to give your views on a controversial subject only to find that the audience you will be facing does not happen to share your opinion. The formula for this situation is moderation. You cannot write a straightforward, hard-hitting speech. You must temper your words and create some sympathy for yourself before you smack them over the head with what you have come to say. Here is a suggested method of procedure:

1. It is difficult to imagine that you and your audience are going to disagree on everything. There must be some common ground. Find it. Find it by talking to representative members of the group or by asking other community leaders.

2. Perhaps the organization you are addressing has once taken a position with which you agree. Start your speech by congratulating them on their farsighted contributions to the community. And be specific about the issue.

3. Remind them that you and they share a common purpose, which is working for the good of the community. Applaud them for being strong-minded and positive.

4. They may disagree with what you are about to say, but this does not mean that they are all impossible to deal with. Single out their leaders and compliment them on their accomplishments.

5. Attack the issue obliquely at first. You and your audience may disagree on the best approach to the issue under discussion, but certainly there are a number of solutions that are unacceptable to you both. Bring these out and dismiss them. They will applaud you because they feel the same way you do.

6. Finally, when you state your own case, you will be talking to an audience that is at least willing to listen. You will

discover that the time you have spent softening them up has been time very well spent, indeed. You may not win them over to your view completely. But you will have successfully introduced a new dimension to their thinking.

The Ceremonial Speech

The greeting card industry in the United States has flourished because a few shrewd observers of the American scene noted our obsession with acknowledging anniversaries, holidays, and days of special significance. Unhappily, we carry this obsession over to our working and social lives. If an employee manages to stay with his company for ten years, the almost universal practice is to honor him with a pin and embarrass him with a speech. Let a group of salesmen surpass a sales quota and the event becomes an occasion marked by oratory. When Founder's Day shows up on the calendar, the church social group can count on some appropriate words by the speaker at their next meeting.

By and large, speeches of this type have a resonating dullness, matched only by the excitement of watching an egg boil. The reason, as should be apparent to all by now, is that there is really very little for the speaker to say. Once he congratulates an individual on his achievement or takes note of an anniversary, he usually branches off in one of two directions—and both are equally disastrous.

He can mouth the same old tired clichés we have all heard dozens of times, on how Mr. Parsons in the traffic department is a symbol of the integrity and hard work that made America the great land it is. Or he can crack some hideous jokes that run like this: "Well, we're here to honor Joe Parsons for ten years of service. I see you showed up in time for the dinner, Joe. Why don't you try being on time for your job, too?" (Weak laughter.) "If you do, maybe we'll give you the next ten-year pin in five years." (Weaker laughter and perhaps a sullen smile from Joe Parsons.)

It is true that most of these ceremonial occasions in business often seem hollow, empty, and a waste of everyone's time. On the other hand, the person or group that is being honored has presumably accomplished something of note and should feel justifiably proud of it. Never lose sight of the fact that Joe Parsons has put ten years of his life working in the traffic department. He feels that the job is a real part of him and, although he might be the last to admit it, he has a sentimental attachment to the company. He deserves better than pompous windbaggery or an insulting attempt at humor.

This is especially true when you're to acknowledge a retirement. Industrial psychologists have pointed out time and again that retirement is a wrenching experience. To put it quite bluntly, many people who retire are filled with despair. They feel their useful life is at an end and that they're being put out to pasture.

Under these circumstances to wisecrack with old Henry in expediting about all the fun he's going to have girl watching in Florida is not only inexcusable, it's cruel.

I once heard of a case where the president of a medium-sized manufacturing company in the Midwest officiated at a retirement presentation for a woman employee who had been with his firm for twenty-two years. Her name was Catherine Brown and she was a widow. According to her fellow employees, her most outstanding characteristics were her gentle, ladylike qualities. They knew she had been widowed at the age of forty after living a life of comparative wealth. Her own family had had money and she went to good schools. In addition, she married money, ran a very comfortable house, and traveled extensively with her husband, who was a prominent physician. About three years after he died, financial reverses ruined her. She had no children and no family. Her answer was to learn shorthand and typing, and she had supported herself as a secretary ever since. Those who worked with her admired her independent spirit and liked her because, as one of the girls put it, "She never tries to impress you with the fact she had money. You can talk to her."

Mrs. Brown had lived a fairly lonely life for the past twenty-two years and, after retirement, would probably live an even lonelier one. The president of the firm, of course, knew nothing of Mrs. Brown's background and was extremely unattractive in his forced heartiness. He peppered his talk with expressions like, "Well we all know there's life in the old girl yet, eh, Katie?" No one had ever called her by anything other than Mrs. Brown. Even her closest friends always referred to her in that formal fashion. Hearing the president call her "Katie" shocked most of the audience and was a deeply disturbing experience for Mrs. Brown. What should have been a warm and memorable tribute turned instead into an ugly memory.

The cardinal rule in preparing a short talk to be given at a retirement dinner or at the presentation of a service award is to take the trouble of inquiring about the individual's background. A few discreet conversations with the personnel department or with long-time associates of the individual to be honored should result in an impression of his personality. Interview some of his superiors and try to draw out anecdotal material that throws light on the kind of person he is and what his contributions to the company have been.

Another story also involves a woman at retirement age. She was a filing clerk who had been at her job for thirty-seven years. She was modest and hardworking and kept her personal life to herself. Very few in the company knew that she had put four sons through college single-handedly. But the president found it out. He admired her accomplishments and felt that hers was a truly useful, rich life. He said so sincerely and simply at her retirement party and everyone there was moved. That woman said later she would never forget her last day on the job and that she would always feel she had friends in the company.

This is the key to writing a ceremonial speech—understand that it is an important occasion for someone present, respect that feeling, and make that person come vividly alive for your audience. This holds equally true whenever you are called upon to recognize an achievement. If a shift maintained an exceptionally high rate of production, or if a group of salesmen performed beyond the norm, find out the character of the men. Find out what obstacles they overcame to achieve their results. They are not, as so many speeches would have it, "representative of the driving force that has contributed to the success of the ABC Company." They are not representative of anything. They are individuals who deserve to be recognized for specific accomplishments. Tell your audience what these accomplishments have been, and turn a ceremony into a meaningful occasion.

Summary

You will have noticed, in this discussion of speeches for the more common occasions, that I have made repeated reference to the importance of relating your remarks to your audience. This theme will reappear over and over again throughout this book because it is perhaps the most useful advice you will ever receive on the subject of preparing a speech. Let's review these speaking situations and the points to remember about each.

1. *Your Occupation.* What you do is of interest to a surprising number of people. You should have many opportunities to talk about your job or profession in public. You will do this before various audiences:

a. *A business occasion:* You are speaking before a group of your peers, all of them as interested in, and perhaps even as informed about, your subject as you are. As a starting point, ask yourself what the most controversial questions are facing your industry. Then make a second list of the innovations or developments that would most benefit your industry. From these two lists, choose a subject.

b. *A church or social group:* Examine where their lives touch your occupation and expand on that relationship. Do not raise controversial issues and, above all, don't become highly technical.

c. *A service organization:* Tell the local Rotary Club how your business contributes to the good of the community. Make the public service side of your occupation the keynote here.

d. *Young people:* Do not lecture, explain, or extoll your occupation. Instead, talk about how it will be changed by their generation. Look to the future and forget about either the present or the past.

2. *Your Interests or Hobbies.* Temper your enthusiasms. It is easy to become carried away when you talk about something that excites you. Exercise restraint and be sure that you have one—and only one—central thesis for your speech.

3. *Community Affairs.* These are usually speeches of an activist nature. Before you rush headlong into taking a firm position, make sure where your audience stands.

a. *A neutral audience:* You can write your speech without worrying unduly about the reaction you are going to get. Do as straightforward and powerful a job of persuading as you can.

b. *A generally sympathetic audience:* Nice to have, but don't let their approval of your point of view lead you into a bombastic oration. Provide them with strong leadership by presenting a carefully reasoned consideration of all the choices open to them, together with what each means.

c. *A hostile audience:* Get them sympathetic before you launch into your main argument. This is perhaps the only case where there is a good excuse for you to delay moving in on your central thesis. Unless you soften them up properly, they will resist your main arguments. Move slowly and practice a little flattery.

4. *The Ceremonial Speech.* Retirements, anniversaries, and the recognition of achievements may be a bore to you, but they are meaningful to those concerned. Take the time and trouble to learn something about the personalities you are honoring. Talk about their accomplishments in a sincere and warm way.

CHAPTER 5

Ghostwriting Is a Scary Business

For perfectly obvious reasons, what goes on between a ghostwriter and his "client" is a private matter, not open for public discussion. While virtually no prominent businessman or political figure writes his own speeches these days, he never admits that fact. You will not find me knocking the system. I've earned my living by it for too long. Besides, there's a perfectly legitimate reason why men who are constantly asked to speak do not do their own writing. They're invited to make a speech because they have made a name for themselves, because they have achieved a certain stature in the eyes of the public. These accomplishments usually come about because of hard work and long hours. This means that most of them simply cannot afford the time to write a polished address. Some of these individuals make a public appearance as often as five or six times a month. The mayor of New York City, for example, regularly has a few words to say to three or four groups a day. Obviously, if he were to pre-

94

pare his remarks himself he wouldn't have any time to do his job. Hence a speech writer, or a "ghost."

The function of a ghostwriter is to interpret the thoughts and ideas of the man actually giving the speech. He must synthesize the speaker's views on the subject and express them in an interesting and forceful fashion that faithfully reflects the speaker's personality. This, alone, makes it a rather difficult job.

But a ghostwriter's craft is the least of it. I have found that, by and large, the trickiest part of a ghostwriter's job is in the area of how he works with his client. The skills can be learned. But he can never anticipate the exact nature of the relationship he will develop with his client. There are, however, a few principles that I have learned—and I still have the scars to prove it—about the curious way a ghostwriter and the man he writes for develop a speech together. I bring the subject up not because I want to train recruits in this arcane art. I'm not interested in nurturing my own competition. This chapter is intended for that unfortunate in the accounting department whose boss has to deliver a talk in three weeks and asks him to prepare "a few notes" for it. These "few notes" mean a full-fledged speech, and the junior accountant had better face up to that fact. He had also better face up to the fact that this innocent-seeming request can easily balloon into a major crisis. Fortunately, there are a few rules that will provide some protection during what is, at best, a very difficult time.

Getting the Assignment

When a professional speech writer is called in for an assignment, there is no question in anyone's mind what he is supposed to do. But very often the call for help takes the form of the boss asking someone in his own department to lend a hand. Take the case of your supervisor poking his head in your doorway and saying, "By the way, Mr. Big wants to see you. He'd like a little help with a presentation he's going to make on the new product line at the West Coast sales conference next month." What exactly does "a little help" mean? You walk into Mr. Big's office puzzled and somewhat unsure of yourself. To compound the difficulty, the chances are that Mr. Big isn't quite sure himself what it is he wants. And this, as any student of the business scene will tell you, is a surefire situation for trouble. Whenever a manager and one of his subordinates collaborate on a project and neither has a clear concept of either the rules of procedure or their common goal, the stage is set for what can become a rather nasty time. Tempers are bound to flare and you end up in an argument with your boss, which is not a particularly productive exchange from your point of view. The most effective way to prevent this from happening is to understand from the beginning what you are expected to do. Then, even if your boss doesn't understand, you will be able to take charge quietly and firmly.

If you are ever asked to "put together a few notes" for your boss, you should bear in mind you've made an impression on him. He chose you and not someone else in the department. Obviously you were tapped for the assignment because he had confidence in you, and if you do a first-rate job his high opinion of you will be reinforced. So look upon a speech-writing assignment as an opportunity, but watch out for the pitfalls.

The Interview

There is a curious fact of life influencing the relationship between the speech writer and his "client" that is widely appreciated within the profession. Most businessmen are uncomfortable at the thought of employing a ghostwriter. For some reason they feel they should be doing it themselves. I think that a businessman tends to feel that he got where he is because of his willingness to do the job himself and turning it over to someone else makes him feel almost guilty. Top executives of large companies quickly get over this complex. They soon realize that their time is better spent with matters of more direct concern to the welfare of their operation. But those in middle management or the infrequent speaker often suffer from a highly ambivalent feeling toward an outsider.

So be aware of this when you walk into Mr. Big's office for the first time. It is not good policy to say cheerfully, "Well, Boss, I hear you want me to write a speech for you." The implication is that you're going to do it for him because he can't do it for himself. The attitude to take instead is that you're there to put together some background material and perhaps develop a few of his ideas. You know, of course, that you're going to write the entire speech, and even he may know it. But maintaining a polite fiction about the process will make your relationship go much more smoothly.

You'll be able to tell within the first few minutes of your interview how your "client" wants to proceed. At one point in my life, over a four-year period with a large corporation I wrote seventeen speeches for the same executive. My job description was that of speech writer. Everyone knew what my function was, so you would think the matter of maintaining a fiction would never arise. But it did. Each time I received a call from this man's secretary, it was "to help do some research for a speech Mr. Blank has to give." And that's the way we always referred to it in our meetings. Beyond establishing the proper relationship, there are a few things you *must* do in order to get matters started on the right foot.

GET THE FACTS

Make sure you understand the nature of the audience your man is addressing, and get it clear in your mind, and his, what sort of occasion it will be. Is it going to be a formal address or just some informal remarks? Both are equally demanding to write, but the tone of your speech will differ with the affair. Try to find out as diplomatically as possible how important the occasion is to the speaker. If he feels his speech is going to enhance his reputation, then you have fair warning that you had better come up with something rather special. However, even if he appears to be casual about the affair, don't make the mistake of treating it as lightly as he does. Underneath his offhanded manner he knows that he is going to be on his feet before a roomful of people, and he certainly wants to be well-prepared.

At the same time, don't leave the room without reaching a full understanding of the subject matter and approach. It's not enough for Mr. Big to say to you, "Listen, Jack, I want to tell the boys out on the West Coast about the new product line. Do you think you can pull some notes together for me?"

Your answer to that should be, "Hey, that's a great idea. We sure have a lot of things to say about the line. Where do you think the emphasis should be?"

This puts the ball squarely back in his court. There are two advantages to this sort of reply. First, it forces your boss to focus his thinking, which will make your job a great deal easier. And second, it gives him the feeling that he is really participating in the speech-writing process, as indeed he is. Do *not* under any circumstances come back with, "Good idea. Now here's the way to tackle it." Let him do the talking. It's his speech, after all, and he should contribute the fundamental ideas.

FIND A FOCUS

Once you've asked your boss where he wants the emphasis to be, don't let him off the hook. Don't accept a vague, "Well, you know the line as well as I do. You know what to say."

Keep the conversation going. Here's how the dialogue could go:

You: I was talking to Herb out in San Francisco just the other day and he said the boys are impressed by the research that went into the line this year.

Boss: You think we ought to lead off with that?

You: Does research sell the product? Do you think it's sexy enough?

Boss: Sure, it's a damn good story.

You: I was thinking about the design.

Boss: Now that's true. It's well-designed, all right.

You: And engineered.

Boss: Yeah, sure is.

You: Say! That's a good idea.

Boss: What is?

You: Making the point that they all contribute to the line. The reason our line is so good this year is because of its balanced strength.

Boss: Balanced strength . . . that's kind of nice.

You: Right. And while we're about it, let's not forget the marketing research that's gone into the line. . . .

Boss: Yes, and advertising and point-of-sale promotion.

You: Good idea. You know, the nice thing about this approach is that you'll be handing out congratulations to every department in the company.

Boss: I think I'll circulate it around and score a few points. OK, I'll hit the theme of balance. See what you can do to develop that idea.

You: What do you think we ought to leave them with?

Boss: I don't follow you.

You: Well, you make the point that the line is great because of the team effort that went into it. That it's got this great balance and everything. . . .

Boss: Yeah. . . .

You: What about goals? What about telling them a wonderful opportunity this year's line represents. . . .

Boss: That it's up to them now to sell the hell out of the product.

You: Right! And that it's going to mean money in their pockets.

Boss: You bet. I want to get those guys so excited about their prospects that they're ready to sell seventy hours a week. That's the way we'll meet quota.

You: Surpass it, you mean.

Boss: That's the ticket. Now, here's what I want you to do. Go around to all the departments and get me the facts on why they think they've done an outstanding job on this year's line. Why it's better than anything we've ever done before—from an engineering standpoint, a design standpoint, and so forth. You understand?

You: Sure.

Boss: We'll put it all together so the message comes through loud and clear that the whole package is the greatest opportunity that's ever come along. And that we expect the best sales year ever. What do you think of that as an idea for the speech?

You: Beautiful, Boss. Just beautiful.

Such a dialogue is a little too perfect ever to be true, but it does serve the purpose of illustrating how you *must* force your "client" into focusing his rather general thoughts. And even more important, how you should try to give the impression that the ideas are his. This isn't just a matter of trying to flatter the boss, although there is an element of that present. If he thinks the ideas are his, he'll be more likely to accept your initial draft and this makes your work much simpler.

STAY IN THE BACKGROUND

Once you've been given your assignment, you will probably be talking to others in the company in order to get the information you need. Be careful when you do. Don't approach the head of another department with a "Listen, I need some help because I'm writing a speech for Mr. Big to give at the sales conference next month." This will immediately get back to Mr. Big, and any feelings of anxiety he might have about employing a ghostwriter will be brought out into the open. Define your role in a more modest manner. Tell him, "Mr. Big asked me to dig out some facts he needs for a speech he's giving." There's nothing wrong with that. It just leaves unanswered the question of authorship.

THE NEXT STEP

Before you leave the first interview, make sure you both know what the next step is. Don't walk out giving the impression that you'll be back with a completed speech. Some businessmen want to see a rough outline first. Others would rather wait to review a detailed plan. Find out which approach your man prefers. But limit it to an outline. It is easier to make changes in an outline than it is in a finished talk. In any event, it is desirable to involve your "client" with every step in the procedure. This participation encourages him to believe that the speech is really his. Incidentally, never deceive yourself that the speech you are writing is yours. Some people wonder if I don't get frustrated when I hear praise heaped on one of my clients for a speech I have written. Of course not. It means I still have a client. Remember that if a speech goes well, it's "his" speech. If it goes badly, then it's your speech.

Your Second Interview

Your second interview pretty well sets the content and form of the speech you are writing. The document you present should be an outline that reflects your judgment of how the ideas discussed in your previous meeting should be organized. I have found it useful, at this stage, to talk through the outline rather than to sit back passively while my client reads through it.

This second interview should deal with every section of the proposed speech. You should make it crystal clear how you intend to develop each argument and how they will all flow together as a whole. Allow your "client" every opportunity to question, evaluate, and even criticize. You will often find, at this point, that the man for whom you are writing will introduce new ideas. This is because he, too, has been thinking about the speech since your last meeting, and he may have altered some of his opinions or thought of a fresh approach which he now thinks is more effective. This is his prerogative. You must learn to be flexible. However, if the new material distorts your central argument, it is your responsibility to point this out. Let's say that you've brought in an initial outline for Mr. Big's talk at the sales conference, and let's continue the dialogue.

Boss: Not bad. But, you know, I've been thinking that we ought to hit them a little harder.
You: How do you mean?
Boss: I mean put the fear of God in them. Ajax is putting out a pretty good line, too. Let them know they're going to have competition. That it's not going to be a piece of cake for them.

You: You want that to be your major theme?
Boss: You bet. Hit 'em right between the eyes with it.

In this imaginary exchange, notice how this new idea distorts the focus of the approach you had previously settled on. Instead of giving the sales conference a positive message of strength, your boss is now proposing to turn it around completely by stressing the power of the competition. In the first version, the speech tried to motivate the salesmen by illustrating all the advantages of the line. It tried to move them by holding out the promise of a dazzling product. In the second version, the motivation is fear. They must work twice as hard because the competition may take the play away from them entirely.

Now, it is not unnatural for Mr. Big to be worried about his competition. During the time that passed between your last meeting and your present one, he must have thought about the competition a great deal and realized that you had made no mention of it in discussing the speech. He clearly thinks this is an oversight and wants it corrected. The only trouble is that he has overreacted and this has blunted the central thrust of the speech. Obviously, you can't tell him that, and you have to find room for his new idea somewhere.

You: That's a good idea. Let's see where we can put it.
Boss: In the beginning. Right up front.
You: Wouldn't that sound like you were a little too worried about Ajax? And you don't want to give that impression, do you?
Boss: I want them to know that Ajax is around.
You: Then why don't you end with it. Lead off from strength with your discussion of how well-balanced we are, just the way you have it now. Then, at the end, when you talk about all the opportunities they have and how the company really expects them to deliver, that's where you can

talk about the competition. It'll give them something to think about.

Boss: Maybe. Yeah, maybe you've got a point.

You: Let's try it that way. If you don't like it, we can always change it.

Boss: All right.

You: OK. I'll leave a copy of the outline with you and I'll put together a rough draft. Then we can take a look at how closely the draft follows the outline.

This last remark on your part is a very effective way to prevent any further changes Mr. Big might have. You leave the meeting with the clear understanding that you are going to proceed on the basis of the outline you have discussed. Later, if he tries to inject some new material, he will have to do so knowing that it is unexpected.

Writing for Another Voice

When you write a speech for another man, it is extremely important to follow the outline you and he have agreed upon. When you write for yourself, you can take certain liberties with the organization and with the ideas. But you cannot afford to present your boss with new concepts—at least not without talking them over with him beforehand.

At one time my professional life crossed that of one of the most talented speech writers I have ever met. His abilities were widely recognized and he wrote for some of the best-known figures in American business and public life. But he never could keep a job. This puzzled me until I heard some-one say, "X is one of the best writers in the business, no question of it. But his trouble is that he always wants to stick in his own ideas. They're damn good ideas, usually, but they just don't happen to be the ones we agreed on. He keeps changing the game."

So, once you've got a firm agreement, and approval of an outline, the wise course is to follow it. Don't think you're doing anyone a favor by coming up with surprises. Stick with the outline and write as simply as you can.

Every man has his own habits and peculiarities whenever he speaks. President Johnson's style was quite different from President Kennedy's. How is it possible, then, to write in another man's style?

I have found that the best solution to this problem is not to think about it. Unless I know a man extremely well, I make no attempt to fashion my sentences in a way that I imagine he will deliver them. There are a few limited exceptions. If I have written a number of speeches for a particular man I will know which words he favors. I may even know that he has trouble with certain words or phrases, and so I naturally avoid these. Beyond that, I merely try for a simple, straightforward style, using relatively short sentences. I do this because I feel that the speaker will put his own imprint on the speech after he receives the first full draft.

The Final Draft

In nine cases out of ten you will find that, if you have developed the speech closely with your boss, there will not be too much trouble with the final draft. You may be dismayed by the number of changes he has made in your text, but you'll discover that they are not substantive. He will substitute one word for another. He may even cross out an entire paragraph because he feels it slows the pace of his ideas. But there should be little or no attempt to introduce entirely new themes that result in unexpected conclusions. These hen scratches over your manuscript are all part of the game. Do not permit yourself the luxury of injured pride of authorship, even if he takes out a phrase you're particularly fond of and replaces it with one of his own. The speaker is merely going through the process of adapting your draft to his own personality.

If, however, the changes depart radically from the basic outline, you should point this out. Remind him that you had agreed on another approach and he may back down. However, if he stands fast, there is little you can do. It is, after all, his speech and not yours. This is bitter medicine for many speech writers to swallow, but they must understand that it is their function to come up with a speech that their man can live with comfortably.

Criticism

Without any question, your boss is going to ask for an outside opinion of his speech. Don't be concerned about this. If he passes it around inside the company the remarks will probably be complimentary. After all, who wants to offend the boss? However, if he gets an evaluation from a source he respects you have to deal with the matter tactfully.

Mr. Big has just received some comments on his speech from Mr. Brown, one of the partners of the CPA firm that does your auditing.

Boss: Look here, Brown thinks we ought to put the marketing effort in the perspective of the larger economic forecasts for the year. He says he's got some material that will be helpful. Why don't you go over and talk to him.

You: That's a good idea. As a matter of fact, we might be able to use that stuff in another version of this same speech.

Boss: Another version! I was thinking about using it now.

You: With all due respect, Brown's a first-class CPA. But does he know our salesmen?

Boss: He said he thought doing it his way would make it

more of a . . . well . . . you know . . . a statesmanlike address.

YOU: He's right. But let's save it for the right occasion. The guys out on the West Coast aren't interested in any broad economic forecast. They want to know about the line and what it's going to mean to them. And that's what you can tell them. God knows Brown can't.

You will find that most outside comments directed at changing the substance of your speech can be dealt with by pointing out that people have a natural tendency to say things their way and from their own point of view. You can acknowledge that the comments have validity but that doesn't mean they are correct or useful for the occasion. Don't be stiff-necked about accepting outside criticism. Give it full marks, but indicate that you don't necessarily think it is appropriate for the speech your boss is working on at the moment. This simple device can save you from the drudgery of starting all over again at the last minute.

Setting Him Up

Professional speech writers are finished with their job when the speech is typed in final form. But not you. You would be wise to double-check all the arrangements surrounding your boss's speaking engagement. Perhaps his secretary has already done so, but don't rely on it. Ask her and if there is any doubt or confusion contact someone from the organization to be addressed. In the case of Mr. Big, someone is running the sales conference. Find out from him when Mr. Big is expected and where he will be met. Find out who will make the introductions and if the meeting is large enough to warrant a microphone. Making certain about these minor details will help insure a successful appearance and, who knows, it may even open up a new career for you as a speech writer. If that happens, my advice to you is to quit.

Summary and Checklist

1. When you're asked to "work up a few notes" for your boss, understand that he's really asking you to write a full speech. Even so, maintain the fiction that you're just lending him a hand.

2. Stay in the background. Don't noise it around that you're writing a speech. The official line is that you are developing some background.

3. Lay down the ground rules for the speech firmly in the first interview. Force your boss to focus his own thoughts about what he wants to say. Hammer out your basic theme and approach right away.

4. Prepare a detailed outline. Talk it through with your boss. Accept any changes he makes, provided they do not change the approach you had previously agreed upon.

5. Give your boss a copy of the revised final outline. Get him to understand that this is the document you will be using as you draw up a preliminary draft.

6. Don't worry about trying to write in another man's style. Express yourself clearly and simply in straightforward prose.

7. Stick to the outline you've agreed upon. Don't throw in new material without first talking it over.

8. Learn to accept changes in the style of your speech gracefully. Question any substantive ones.

9. Be prepared for criticism from outsiders and develop a way to blunt it diplomatically.

10. Double-check all the details that surround the speaking engagement. Make sure your boss knows what is expected of him.

11. Don't make the mistake of coming to believe that this is "your" speech. If you write for someone else, it's all his.

Part II

On Your Feet

CHAPTER 6

Before You Speak

It's finished at last, well in advance of your speaking engagement. But if you think there's nothing more to be done
until the moment arrives, you're quite mistaken. There are
still a number of decisions to make and details to attend to.
These may seem routine and hardly worth the effort, but in
public speaking, as in any other enterprise, it's the details
that can often spell the difference between failure and success. Take a hint from the pros—the men and women on the
lecture circuit. One of the services they demand from the
bureau that arranges their tour is a complete picture of what
to expect when they arrive. They do not relish surprises.

In the days when Joan Crawford's husband was the chairman of the board of the Pepsi Cola Company, she undertook
regular personal appearances and speaking trips for the firm.
As a well-known movie star she was accustomed to appearing in public, so her talk was never a problem. Audiences
were invariably charmed by her wit and femininity. But har-
ried members of the Pepsi Cola public relations staff, who
were responsible for her travel arrangements, recall that she

was fanatical about details. She insisted on knowing absolutely everything about her forthcoming appearances. What was the name of the meeting chairman? Where did he go to school and what were his interests? Was he married? Had he ever been divorced? What was the name of his wife? The names of his children? Miss Crawford studied photographs so that she knew the names of people before she even met them. The dossier she insisted upon would have done credit to the Russian secret police. What's more, she remembered it all, and woe to the hapless PR man who told her the chairman's wife's name was Betty when it actually was Judy. When confronted with what she considered to be such gross negligence, she became as feminine as an enraged tigress.

But even those who had felt her claws grudgingly admitted that things rarely went wrong when she appeared to deliver a talk. She knew exactly what was expected of her. She had an encyclopedic knowledge of her audience and such a clear idea of where she would be and what she would be doing every minute of the time that it all appeared to happen easily and spontaneously.

Spontaneity often requires an enormous amount of effort, and there are few who can afford the staff Miss Crawford employed to make it possible. But her insistence upon thorough preparation serves to illustrate an important point. Joan Crawford had no problem in drawing an audience. People gladly came to see and meet such a famous personality. It was not really necessary for her to take such preliminary pains to insure a successful appearance. But take them she did, and, as a result, a pleasantly successful occasion became a triumph both for her and for the company she was representing. She was one of the most effective goodwill ambassadors any business enterprise ever had, and Pepsi Cola gladly paid her not inconsiderable expenses.

Short of hiring a full-time staff, it is impossible for the average speaker to duplicate this effort. But there are certain precautions he can and should take. There is information he should acquire, and certain routine questions to be asked before making any speech. Strict adherence to this policy is your guarantee of staying out of easily avoided trouble. A man loses all of his dignity and most of his effectiveness when he slips on the banana peel he never knew was there because he hadn't bothered to inquire.

Know Your Hall

Quite often you will be asked to speak in an auditorium or meeting room that is familiar to you. But occasionally you may have to travel to another city to speak before a group in a setting you have never seen before. This can present problems, especially if it is a rather formal evening affair. At these occasions the physical layout can be unsettling. It is not unusual for there to be one, two, or even three dais tables. The hotel often provides what amounts to stage lighting and, of course, loudspeakers have been strung throughout the room. Under these conditions, the journey from your place at the dais table to the lectern can be a hazardous one. The area through which you pass can be a jungle of lighting and microphone cable, so you must pick your way carefully.

In addition, a spotlight can momentarily blind you. Not so long ago, the principal speaker at a chamber of commerce dinner in a midwestern city rose to his feet to acknowledge his introduction, stepped back from his chair, and abruptly vanished from sight. The audience, which had been expecting a description of how new businesses were being attracted to the community, was not prepared for a magic act. They gasped with astonishment. A moment later, the speaker emerged from behind the dais table slightly disheveled, his notes in disarray. He had been done in by three steps that led up to the platform supporting his table. Everyone in the room found the situation enormously amusing. But not the speaker. Unable to compete with the waves of suppressed laughter that came from all parts of the room, he cut short his remarks and returned to his seat in a cold rage. Just as he was climbing back up on the platform a voice from the audience shouted out, "Play it again, Sam!" This brought down the house and signaled the end of any serious business that night.

If you are to speak in unfamiliar surroundings, try to get an idea of the layout. The program chairman can help you. Find out from him exactly where you'll be sitting. Don't assume you'll be leaving your seat to speak from a lectern. You may be expected to rise and talk from your place. Get the facts. And don't forget to inquire about microphone arrangements. You will probably encounter only three basic types— a standing mike which presents problems because it can screen you from your own notes, a desk mike attached to the lectern, or a microphone that loops around your neck and gives you total freedom of motion. It's important to know the kind you will be expected to use because it can alter your delivery.

Some time ago, I wrote a speech for a business executive who assumed he would be confronted with a desk microphone on a lectern. Instead, he found a neck microphone which he had never before used. This gave him so much trouble that his speech was delayed nearly a full minute. A minute of silence, relieved only by some labored breathing and the sight of a man struggling unsuccessfully to loop a wire around his neck, is at least an eternity. The audience was pulling for him, though, and when an involuntary "damn" came booming hoarsely over the public address system they responded with encouraging applause and laughter. Fortunately, my man had enough poise to turn the situation to his advantage. He cheerfully admitted defeat and proceeded to deliver his talk with the neck microphone clutched in his right hand. For a less-experienced speaker, such an incident might not have turned out so happily.

Of course, even the best-informed program chairman will not have every last detail at his fingertips. So look around carefully before it's time for you to speak. Chart the quickest, least cluttered route to the speaker's platform, and cast a wary eye out for obstacles such as steps half hidden in darkness or a tangle of electrical wiring. Your audience may want to be entertained, but not at your expense.

Know the People

When you speak in public, you will not suddenly appear before an audience like a phoenix risen. You will be surrounded by people; there will be a chairman to conduct the meeting, and some member of the group may be assigned the task of introducing you. If the occasion involves a dinner, you will probably mingle with the other honored guests at a reception, and you will certainly pass the entire evening seated between two of them. All of these people might very well turn out to be perfect strangers, and yet the rules of the game require you to be sociable with all of them. The spectacle of a line of silent dais guests, each munching morosely on his chicken without any attempt at small talk, is likely to depress even the most lively audience.

Making small talk with strangers can be awkward—but only if you know nothing about them. If a well-run organization invites you to speak, the chances are that at least two members will be assigned to convoy you through the evening. They will make it their business to know something about you, and they will be prepared to lead the conversation around to your particular interests and hobbies.

But don't count on this personalized service. Find out something about your fellow guests, and be especially sure to learn the names of your dinner mates. It is a good idea to write these people in advance, expressing your anticipation of the evening ahead. You may not mean a word of it, but it is only common courtesy, and it will help you through the dinner more smoothly. They will be delighted by your thoughtfulness and redouble their efforts to make you feel at ease.

It is absolutely essential for you to know the name of the individual who will introduce you, for you will have to acknowledge him in your opening remarks. "Thank you, Mr. Smith, for your gracious words of introduction," can lead to an icy stare if he happens to be Dr. Smith. Titles are important.

At the same time, the chairman of the meeting may want you to acknowledge the presence of some distinguished guests. Even if it is an informal affair, take nothing for granted. Ask him. An extremely formal affair virtually requires that this protocol be observed. At a university commencement it is more appropriate to begin your speech with, "Mr. President, Senator Smith, Dr. Brown, distinguished members of the faculty, ladies and gentlemen," than it is to start out with a cheery, "Good morning, folks."

These rules may seem simple and self-evident. If they are, so much the better. Unfortunately, however, many inexperienced speakers tend to overlook them. The experienced ones do not. They have learned that walking into a dinner sponsored by a group of strangers is a little like traveling in a foreign country. It's easy to make the natives hostile and to create a state of mutual embarrassment.

Your Props

The most common prop used by speakers is the microphone, and it can create special problems for the uninitiated. Ideally, a speaker should be given a chance to test his microphone and sound equipment before the audience has gathered. Since this almost never happens, he must experiment with his mike technique at the outset of his talk. Because of wide differences among sound systems, this will seldom be the same twice.

There are very few absolute rules set forth in this book, but here is one to follow if you value your audience: Start out at a sound level you think may be too low, and then increase your volume slowly as you draw closer to the microphone. Shouting with the microphone almost touching your lips can blow your listeners out of their seats. In addition, you are inviting feedback—which results in an ear-splitting electronic whine.

It is difficult for a speaker to determine optimum level because he hears the sound differently than his audience does. And the larger the hall, the more difficult this becomes. Some speakers station their wives, or an associate, in the rear of the hall to act as a sort of "sound spotter." A simple hand signal can tell the speaker to lower or increase his volume. If that isn't practical for you, keep an eye on the people in the back rows. If they're straining forward, you're not getting through to them. If they're cringing in their seats, you're overwhelming them.

Few speeches need any props other than a microphone. If you feel you must have additional audiovisual aids, review your talk carefully. Perhaps you can simplify and clarify, so that your words alone carry the full meaning of what you say. Generally speaking, I do not like speakers who use flip charts on an easel or depend upon slide projectors.

There are two reasons for this. First, it dilutes the rapport that should be carefully built between a speaker and his audience. If a speaker dims the lights to show a slide, his presence vanishes; the audience can no longer see him, they merely hear him. When the lights come back on, contact has to be reestablished. Second, speakers often use audiovisual devices as a crutch. Some become so enamored with slide and film-strip trickery that they end up with a presentation that resembles a mixed-media show, much to the confusion of everyone present. If graphic aids are absolutely essential —and I grant they sometimes are—keep them simple and try to bunch them together. Avoid the habit of switching lights on and off throughout your talk. There's little to be gained by forcing your audience to blink like owls for half an hour.

Above all, if you use audiovisual devices, have the slides or film strips prepared by an expert. A graph that has great meaning for you can easily be incomprehensible to an audience lacking your expertise. AV specialists are aware of this and are trained to present your graphic material clearly and simply.

Finally, know your equipment. There is nothing so disconcerting for an audience as sitting in the dark waiting for the speaker to find the right switch. Practice working your equipment beforehand, and be sure to rehearse your show thoroughly. This is doubly important if you use an assistant. He should have a copy of your manuscript, properly marked so that he clicks the button dead on cue. Do not rely on a volunteer who offers his services an hour before you're to deliver your talk. Confusion will almost invariably result, and what could have been a pleasant friendship will deteriorate into a snarling match.

The Importance of Rehearsal

Actors complain they never have enough rehearsal time, and I wish more public speakers felt the same way. But even more important than time spent is the quality of the rehearsal itself. Rehearsal does not simply mean reading over your speech. It means concentrated work, thinking how each paragraph sounds, and then trying to project its impact on an imaginary audience. It means experimenting with various ways of phrasing, with different patterns of vocal inflection. It means deciding where pauses are most effective, and then marking them down on your manuscript.

Actors do not rehearse by sitting down and exchanging their lines. Body movements are an important part of their craft, and they practice these endlessly. So should public speakers. Get up out of your chair in front of a mirror. Watch yourself, keeping an eye on your facial expressions and your hand motions. Even the most experienced speaker can become tangled when he uses his hands. During the presidential elections of 1968, a national magazine, admittedly somewhat critical of Richard Nixon, reported that he suffered from a certain confusion on the platform. The article singled out an instance when Mr. Nixon said to his audience, "And *I* offer my pledge to *you* . . . ," gesturing to his audience when he came to the word *I* and back to himself when he forcefully hit the word *you.*

Some speakers make marginal notes to help them with their dramatic effects. Scattered throughout their speech will be admonitions such as, "Slow down here" or "Look grave" or "Pound lectern for emphasis." This is fine if it helps, but with practice you'll soon learn the appropriate gesture.

The use of a tape recorder in rehearsing your speech will probably be a revelation. No one really has any idea of what he sounds like to another, and hearing your own voice through a loudspeaker often comes as a shock. To your surprise, you may find that you're rushing your speech and that your words have a tendency to slur together. Or you may discover that your delivery is halting and unconsciously filled with "ers" and "ahs"—a very common failing. A tape recorder can help you correct your faults and improve your platform manner.

However, if no tape recorder is available, practice on your wife, your secretary, or your unsuspecting brother-in-law. If none of these are willing to serve, rehearse in front of your dog, or, failing that, set up a chair and pretend it is the audience. Above all, do it on your feet exactly as you'll be doing it in actual performance. A lazy rehearsal is no rehearsal at all.

To Read or Not to Read

The decision of whether or not to speak from a prepared text is a question that does not present a problem to the man who is at home on a platform. He has long ago determined the course that works best for him. But many first-time speakers agonize over this decision, principally because there is such conflicting advice on the question. I have four books on public speaking in my library. Two of them state unequivocally that the reader should never, under any circumstances, even consider committing his speech to memory. The other two express total disdain for the speech that is read. It is wooden and ineffective, they argue, and to deliver a speech in such a manner is far worse than giving no speech at all.

It is true that a read speech frequently sounds mechanical. Without the proper rehearsal it reduces the opportunity for the total communication that is so essential between the speaker and his audience. On the other hand, memory can play strange tricks, as the most experienced and well-drilled actors will ruefully admit. Even if this were not the case, the awful specter of going blank in the middle of a sentence can easily reduce an already nervous public speaker into a state of hysterical anxiety. This, of course, virtually guarantees a memory lapse somewhere along the line.

Personally, I am convinced that the decision depends largely on the speaker's preference and experience. It makes absolutely no sense to insist on memorizing a speech when there is even a remote chance of disaster. However, if memorization presents no great psychological barriers, then it should certainly be attempted. There is no question that a speaker, addressing his audience directly without a text, sounds more spontaneous and dynamic. If he does it easily, his listeners are impressed because they are aware he is not speaking from notes, and this implies a self-confidence they admire, as well as a command of subject matter they cannot help but respect. But to jeopardize an entire performance for the sake of a rigidly held opinion is fair neither to the speaker nor to his audience. It causes needless embarrassment to both sides and renders meaningless an occasion upon which a large amount of effort and interest may have been spent.

While I am not inclined to be doctrinaire on the subject, I do not recommend that a first-time speaker deliver his speech from memory. Even if he is fortunate enough to have the gift of total recall, there are too many other things for him to think about. A circus acrobat can feel perfectly confident when he practices walking over a tightrope strung a foot or so above the ground. But the first time he does it in actual performance, dozens of feet in the air, he had better have a net.

Later on, as a speaker gains the confidence that only experience can give him, let him try speaking without notes. But even then, the first attempt should be before a small group of people he knows.

How Do You Like It Typed?

The way a speech is to be typed is really a matter of personal preference. It is usually done either in manuscript form on regular 8½ x 11 paper or on a numbered set of 3 x 5 index cards. In either case, all copy should be triple-spaced. Anything closer together tends to confuse the reader. Typewriters with extra large type are available. Known as jumbo, this type is designed especially for speeches. A local typewriter sale and rental establishment may carry such machines in stock. If you want to feel like a real professional, by all means rent one. But in general they are an optional extra not worth the expense and trouble.

In practice, a formal speech meant to be read from a lectern is generally typed in manuscript form. For a more casual address, where the speaker intends to move about freely, index cards are easier to handle. They can be held in a cupped hand, with the speaker shuffling each card to the bottom of the deck when he's through with it. They act more as reminders than a full text, and are especially useful when a speaker elects to talk from an outline, with key phrases acting as triggers for his oratory. A word of caution on index cards, however; since they are not fastened together, a clumsy move could scatter them on the floor.

To determine your preference, persuade your secretary (or your wife) to type your first speech both ways. Try them alternately when you rehearse, and you will quickly discover which one best suits your particular style.

Last-Minute Insurance

It is remarkable how speakers—particularly those with little experience—forget insignificant details that later balloon into full-fledged crises. Here are three of them worth remembering.

First: In the initial flush of receiving your invitation to speak, did you ask whether the affair would be formal or informal? If you're to speak during the day, dress will almost surely be informal. But you never can tell about an evening function. In today's casual world, a dinner engagement doesn't necessarily mean black tie. If the invitation doesn't specify the type of dress, you'd be wise to ask.

Second: Your good wife. What happens to her? Does she join you on the dais or will she be seated at a special hospitality table? Perhaps no one expected her. If not, she won't appreciate the sudden fumble of attention when she appears.

Neither will you. Neither will the program chairman. Make a note to ask about your wife.

Third: As one of the speakers, you may not have a regular ticket to the event. Is there a reception first? If so, where do you meet? I know of one speaker who wandered forlornly through the dozens of public rooms in a big city hotel searching for his party. When he finally appeared at the doors of the main ballroom, he was stopped because he had no ticket. When he tried to explain to the security officer that he was one of the scheduled speakers, the guard nabbed him as a gate crasher. Fortunately the lost speaker persisted, and soon a nervous dinner committeeman arrived just in time to spring him from the clutches of the law. Check full details of time and place. The name of the hotel and the function are not enough.

Checklist

In fact, early in the week before your engagement it is a good idea to make a final checklist, covering all the points that might otherwise escape your attention. This list should include:

1. *The Hall:*
a. Where will you be seated?
b. Where will you speak?
c. Will there be a lectern?
d. How big is the hall?
e. How large an audience is expected?
f. Will there be a microphone?
g. If so, what type?

2. *The People:*
a. Who is the meeting chairman?
b. Who will introduce you?
c. Who are your fellow dais guests?

d. Who will be sitting next to you during dinner?
e. Must you acknowledge anyone in the opening of your remarks?

   3. *Your Props:*
a. Is your audiovisual equipment in working order?
b. Can you operate it blindfolded?
c. Have you rehearsed with your assistant?
d. Are your visual aids clear?
e. Do they really help your speech?

   4. *Your Speech:*
a. Have you rehearsed it?
b. Have you rehearsed it standing up?
c. Have you experimented with different ways of reading it?
d. Have you rehearsed it in front of your wife?
e. In front of a mirror?
f. With concentration?
g. Have you heard your own voice on tape?
h. Have you had it typed to your satisfaction?

   5. *Your Arrival:*
a. Are you properly dressed?
b. Do you know what happens to your wife?
c. Does she know?
d. Where do you go?
e. What time are you expected?
f. Whom do you ask for?

If you're entirely happy with the answers to all of these questions, you can leave for your speaking engagement secure in the knowledge that you've almost nothing left to worry about as you make your debut in public.

CHAPTER 7

The Perils and Pitfalls

Thanks to the guidelines set down in Part I of this book, you've equipped your finished speech with a surefire, attention-grabbing opener. You've followed through with a forceful expression of your main argument. Your language is lean and graphic, your logic impeccable. Notice the deceptive ease with which you have presented well-chosen, concrete examples that support your principal thesis. No bumpy patches have been allowed to distract your listeners as you move them smoothly along from one thought to the next. Transitional paragraphs are stitched into place so the seams don't show. On the journey to your persuasive conclusion, you have neatly nipped off all opportunities for disagreement. The tone of your speech is exactly right—not professorial or condescending, but neither is it simplistic. You have shown respect for your audience, but at the same time you have made them understand that you are the one in control of the facts and have something of value to communicate to them. Best of all, you've managed to spice a page or two with

125

a couple of anecdotes that brought a thin smile to your wife's face even after your third rehearsal at home.

Beyond that, you've prepared yourself thoroughly for your engagement. You've double-checked date, time, and place with the meeting chairman, and you know it's a black tie affair, so there's no danger of disgracing yourself by showing up in brown shoes. You know who will be introducing you, and you're prepared to acknowledge him by name, and even by title if he's got one. You've staked out the equipment, and, if you're to use a microphone, you know whether it's a hand mike, one on a stand, or the kind you tie around your neck. You have a rough idea of the size of the hall and the size of the audience you can expect. You know if you'll be speaking from your place at the dais table or if you'll have to walk to a lectern. You're aware of the three steps leading down from the main table, so you won't start out by sprawling headfirst in front of your audience. As one of the speakers, you won't be moving in with the other ticket-holders but will meet separately, possibly for a reception, and you've got all that information jotted down.

In addition, you've sized up your audience carefully. You're aware of their interests and, if your topic is at all controversial, you know their leanings. If there is a question-and-answer period, you have a general idea of the kind of questions that will probably be tossed your way, and your scrupulous research has given you confidence that you can field most if not all of them.

With such exhaustive, painstaking preparation, is there anything that could possibly go wrong?

Yes. You could give a bad performance. It would probably not be a disaster, considering the care you have already taken. But unless you have such a towering reputation in your field that no one would dream of questioning the value of what you say, the way you say it can dull your audience, render your points meaningless, and eliminate you forever as a speaking candidate for other meetings. Chairmen have a way of trading this sort of information, and the word quickly gets out on who to avoid at all costs.

If this sounds like rather a bleak observation, and you're wondering why you took the trouble of learning how to write a lively speech when you still have a good chance of looking like a total idiot on the platform, consider the fix you'd be in without all the preliminary work you've invested. Make no mistake, the time you spent organizing your remarks and committing them to paper is essential. It is precisely here where the greatest number of public speaking failures occur. However, once you have gone to the trouble of mastering your material and doing a difficult job well, you would be doing yourself and your subject an injustice by making anything less than a first-rate presentation.

Besides, you can take comfort in the fact that once you've written your speech you've mastered the hardest part of the task. Learning to speak effectively is much easier than learning to write effectively. There are really only a limited number of points to bear in mind. Perhaps the obstacle that looms highest is stage fright.

Stage Fright

Without exception, every manual on public speaking sooner or later gets around to a discussion of fear and its effects on the speaker. Generally, there are two schools of thought on the subject. The first sternly urges you to disregard fear. It advises you that you have nothing to be nervous about. After all, you have been asked to appear presumably because you are more familiar with your subject than any member of your audience is, and if you've done your homework properly all you have to do is speak out. They'll hang on to your every word.

The other school takes a position more in keeping with

reality. It sympathizes with your nervousness and tells you it is the most natural feeling in the world. Every speaker, every performer since the dawn of time has been gripped by stage fright to some degree, so you might as well learn to live with it. Actually it is an ally, and you should make use of it. A certain amount of nervousness before a public appearance, you are told, is an excellent thing. It sends the adrenalin rushing through your system and you are, therefore, more alert and more likely to give a more exciting performance.

I am convinced that the truth about stage fright lies somewhere between these two rather arbitrary positions. You are never going to eliminate fear entirely and, despite all the assurances to the contrary, you are not really going to look upon it as your friend and ally.

The "learn-to-master-your-fears" approach insists that you look at your problem in a detached and logical fashion. The audience *has* come to hear you. You *do* know your subject. You *have* rehearsed it thoroughly. You *know* what you have to say is interesting. So what's there to be afraid of? If you're uneasy, you're being unrealistic. Experience will quickly demonstrate that you can talk to yourself patiently like this for hours and still not do away with your nervousness. There may be no concrete reason on earth why you should be nervous, but your knees will still tremble when you get to your feet. You may be annoyed with yourself for your woeful lack of control, but there's not much you can do about it.

The air traveler may know that statistics clearly show that his is the safest means of transportation. In terms of passenger miles, nothing can match the safety record of commercial aviation. Nevertheless, it is the rare passenger who doesn't get an uneasy feeling in the pit of his stomach as his plane hurtles down the runway toward take-off. There is no longer anything he can do to change his situation. He has committed himself to the flight, and the laws of probability suggest only the minutest chance of mishap. Under these circumstances, it is totally unrealistic of him to feel a twinge of fear.

Irrational or Just Unrealistic?

And yet is it entirely unrealistic? After all, accidents *do* occur, and we read about air fatalities regularly in our newspapers. And so, while the chance of disaster is remote, it is still undeniably true that it exists. This suggests that the sudden moment of quiet panic that grips the airline passenger is not so much unrealistic as it is irrational.

In the case of the public speaker, careful preparation should eliminate all the real fears. He should be able to convince himself that the speech he is carrying to the lectern is an effective one. But that does not do away with all the nagging doubts that inevitably beset him. He *could* drop his notes. He *could* lose his place and thrash about helplessly in an attempt to relocate it. He *could* be suddenly seized by a coughing fit. These eventualities are unlikely to occur and to entertain them at all is perhaps unrealistic. But they are not as irrational as the get-tough-with-fear school suggests. So when you find yourself nervous as you approach the moment of truth on a platform, don't kick yourself mentally for being a fool. You are being a bit irrational, but then neither perfection nor dispassionate logic has ever been noted as a particularly consistent human characteristic.

Besides, there is another very real reason for you to feel anxious before an audience. In today's corporate bureaucratically oriented world, responsibility tends to be diffused. If you are a member of a committee, it is the group that makes the decision, not the individual. If you concur with a proposal in a memorandum, yours will not be the only initials on the bottom of the page. Such comfortable protection is denied you when you speak in public. For a moment in time, you, and you alone, are the focus of attention. The ideas, the method of presentation, and the conclusion are all your responsibility. You cannot hide behind a group, a committee, or a paper wall of interoffice correspondence. It is a terribly lonely feeling and, in a sense, one that weighs even more heavily on a public speaker than it does on any other kind of performer.

An actor and a public speaker share a perfectly justifiable dread of failure. Both are human beings with egos to protect. And yet both choose to expose these easily bruised egos to public judgment. For both, a poor performance is unbearable to contemplate, and the anxiety they feel is not surprising. But actors are relieved of any responsibility for what they say. That rests on the shoulders of the playwright. They are judged only on how imaginatively and excitingly they portray their characters and deliver the writer's lines.

Admittedly these are not inconsiderable accomplishments, but in the case of a speaker, he is appraised not only on the basis of what he says but on how effectively he says it. Such a combination puts any public speaker in an unusually vulnerable position and to pretend that his anxieties and fears are unjustified and therefore unrealistic is not especially helpful. It is unreasonable to expect any speaker to suppress his fears completely. There are too many good reasons for them to exist.

Can You Learn to Use Fear?

On the other hand, pretending that fear is a useful friend has a sort of *Rebecca of Sunnybrook Farm* ring to it that is not very helpful either. The "dignity of the working man" has a rather different meaning for the miner toiling underground for twelve hours a day than it does for the politician engaged in Labor Day oratory. The politician isn't faced with the prospect of spending his days several hundred feet below the surface, and the man who advises you to find profit from fear doesn't have to deliver your speech.

As any actor will readily testify, stage fright is a miserable experience. It is true that the adrenalin-producing quality of nervousness is an asset. But stage fright also contributes to bodily tension. It tightens the muscles, particularly the vocal cords, leading to an unnaturally thin and shaky voice. It causes shortness of breath and it has a disastrous effect on the bladder. To pretend these are assets is foolish. There is simply no way to learn to "use" fear productively.

Can anything be done about stage fright? Unfortunately, not about the fright itself. But its effects can be made less harmful by a few exercises. Before speaking, fill your lungs and diaphragm with as much air as they can hold. Let the air escape slowly and repeat this several times. You'll find this will help steady your nerves, and shortness of breath will not be a major problem when you start to speak. At the same time, stretch your shoulder, chest, and back muscles. You can even do this discreetly in your seat, and it will do much to relax you. Beyond that, there is only one word of comfort. Stage fright almost never remains with you once you are safely launched into your speech. Its most awful moments occur just before you rise. However, as soon as you are past the first page of your text and are fully warmed to your subject your nervousness will vanish. Once you're finished, you'll look back on your experience and say, "Well, that wasn't so bad. I wonder why I was so tight?" You'll wonder until it's time for you to speak again. Then, despite your previous performance, stage fright will grip you once more. It's part of the price paid by anyone who appears before the public. It becomes more manageable with time, but it's ever present. The only thing you can do about it is to learn to live with it in the knowledge that you will give a good performance despite it.

Tension

Ours is a tense society, there's no question of that. Our television screens and the pages of our leading magazines are filled with earnest-looking men in white jackets telling us how important it is for us to relax. Along with the common cold, nervous tension is the leading ailment of our age.

As you read these lines, you may think that you are not particularly keyed up. But try this as an experiment. Put down the book for a moment and lean back in your chair. Close your eyes and form a mental image of your body, starting with the top of your scalp. Then think consciously of the muscles around your eyes, your cheeks, and your mouth. Concentrate on relaxing each set of muscles, and continue on down to your ankles and feet. Do this slowly; the entire operation should take several minutes. You will be surprised at how much "give" there is in every muscle of your body, even at a time of comparative repose. The most effective way of trying this experiment is flat on your back. But don't do it at the office. Your secretary may come in and call an ambulance.

If you're so "up-tight" at a quiet moment like this, imagine the tensions that build up in your body when you rise to speak. As concerned as you are with the occasion, you will probably not be aware of the tension. But it is there and it costs you a tremendous amount of energy. I once wrote for a very prominent businessman who made frequent speeches and who was considered effective on the platform. And so he was. But he had never learned to relax when he spoke in public. When he finished speaking he was, quite literally, exhausted and drenched in perspiration, as if he had just gone through a brisk physical workout. Whenever he spoke before a group at a hotel, a room would be reserved for him where he could retire after his appearance. His postspeaking ritual consisted of a shower, a brief nap, and a complete change of linen.

There are, of course, any number of exercises recommended for this condition. They involve such movements as rotating your shoulders, then suddenly relaxing your neck muscles entirely so that your head drops on your chest like a lead weight. I have heard one expert suggest that you lie flat on your back on the floor, blowing a feather in little puffs through your lips.

The only trouble with these exercises is that you can't perform them when you're really tense. The muscles don't tighten up at home; they begin to lock in when you're on the platform. Rotating your shoulders and bobbing your head up and down violently is hardly acceptable behavior in public. And blowing a feather through your lips while you're flat on your back may just strike your audience as a little peculiar, to say nothing of the others on the platform with you.

But you can practice the exercise I suggested earlier anywhere and at any time, even on a platform waiting for the introduction to your speech. Try to forget about the audience for a few moments and consciously relax your body, muscle by muscle. Breathe regularly and deeply, not exaggerated inhalation but slowly and steadily. When the moment of truth arrives and you move to the podium, your muscles will probably stretch tight like bundles of rubber bands. But at least you will have started from a point of nearly total relaxation and the chances are you will not be quite as tense as you would have been without going through the exercise.

Tight Throat and Stiff Jaw

When you go through your relaxing routine, be sure to pay particular attention to the muscles of your throat and jaw. Read a sentence from this page as you would normally speak in a conversational tone. Now make an effort to tighten your throat and jaw muscles as stiffly as you can. Repeat the sentence out loud. Notice the difference. The sound you have produced is mechanical and hard. There is virtually no resonance in the tone of your voice. This happens to many speakers, and quite often they are not aware of it. Actually, this unpleasant sound occurs because most speakers have not been trained in the fundamentals of vocal production. Unfortunately, the exercises required to develop this skill can only be practiced at home. And so, for the conscientious, a brief section on the mechanics of developing a well-controlled speaking voice.

Your Voice and How It's Produced

Sound is produced when the vocal cords in your throat are set into vibration by a column of air passing through them. It follows then that the more control a speaker has over the column of air, the more control he has over the sound he produces. However, full breath control means learning an entirely new way of breathing. Most of us, when we begin to speak, instinctively fill our lungs with air. This reservoir of compressed air is the motor that drives the speaking mechanism. But it is a most inadequate one because it is rather difficult to control. Far more complete control comes if we concentrate on our diaphragm instead of our lungs. The diaphragm is that part of the body lying between the rib cage and lungs and the abdomen.

Try this experiment in breath control. Stand perfectly straight, suck in your stomach, and fill your lungs with air. Now release the air and make a sustained "aahhhh" sound. You should experience a little trouble controlling volume and tone.

Now repeat the experiment, but instead fill your diaphragm with air. If you are doing this correctly, it will seem as though you are filling your stomach with air, inflating it as you would a balloon. Next, release the air by opening your throat and pushing in with your stomach muscles. You have now created a column of air that extends from your belt to your throat. Control is entirely exercised by your stomach muscles and not by your throat. At first, this will seem artificial and difficult. But if you're really serious about achieving well-rounded and controlled vocal production, you will have to practice it. As a bonus, once you've mastered the technique you will never again suffer from hoarseness or a sore throat because of too much talking or shouting. This is the reason that a baby can cry and even shriek for hours without becoming hoarse. A baby naturally uses his diaphragm and this takes away all pressure from his throat and vocal chords. So this is a skill that must be relearned and, quite frankly, it takes many hours of practice before it comes easily. Only you can decide if you feel it is worth it.

Diction

Good diction was once considered to be as essential to an individual's education as Latin or Greek. By "good" the standards were understood to mean the diction of the upper class. This was particularly true in England and to a lesser degree in the United States. Today, however, good diction no longer means the cultivation of an accent. It means instead the elimination of sloppy, careless speech. A regional accent, whether it's the clipped nasality of Boston or the rolling drawl of Georgia, is perfectly all right provided that the words are not run together or word endings swallowed and garbled. Good diction should be cultivated only for the sake of making yourself intelligible to your audience and avoiding certain patterns that could irritate them.

Usually there is no need to go to a speech coach for advice. Put yourself on tape by reading several articles from the newspaper into a home recorder. Then listen carefully when you play it back. You'll soon spot any areas of weakness you might have. Make a note of these and repeat them, listening to the tapes again and again until they are no longer a problem.

CHAPTER 8

Your Performance

None of the details that we have been discussing will be evident, by themselves, to your audience when you speak. Instead, they will judge you on your overall performance. Concertgoers are not interested in how well or easily the violinist can play difficult scales. They are interested only in the finished product—the way he plays the music they have come to hear.

Similarly, your audience doesn't care how often you've practiced breath control or if you've worked hard to improve your diction. They judge you on your performance.

Mannerisms

Many speakers quite unconsciously develop mannerisms that can distract and irritate an audience. I once listened to a speaker who had a habit of scratching the top of his head in a sort of abstracted manner as he spoke. It looked as though he were conducting a furtive search for dandruff, and we all watched him in fascination. So absorbed were we by his performance that I don't think any of us really understood what he was trying to tell us.

We all develop mannerisms the way a ship builds up barnacles. They don't spring up overnight, but once they've taken root they're extremely difficult to get rid of. They become so much a part of our nature that we do not even think about them. For that reason it is virtually impossible for us to break out of our mannerisms without outside help. Ask your wife or an associate to be absolutely frank about any habits you may have acquired. The wife of a man I once knew told him that he invariably wagged a finger at everyone he spoke to. He even did it to her and, while she had learned to live with it, she thought it a gesture to be avoided whenever he spoke in public. The man was astonished. He was entirely unaware of what had become a totally unconscious habit. Mannerisms should be eliminated. An audience tends to pay more attention to them than to what you are saying.

Use Your Personality

The oil company executive who cautioned me against writing jokes for him because, as he said, "I'm not a funny man," recognized the limitations of his own personality. But personality is not usually so limited. A man can be essentially lighthearted and happy. But that does not mean he never has a serious moment. He may have the reputation of a flip jokester. But he can be earnest, too. Each side of a man's personality should be expressed, in turn, depending upon the circumstances of what he is trying to say, and each is equally valid.

Try to express as many sides of your personality as your speech warrants. Certainly, one of the more attractive qualities that will appeal to most audiences is that of sincerity. An audience is reassured by the sincerity of a speaker. By that I don't mean heaviness or pomposity. I mean a straightforward delivery when the content of your speech seems to require it. Do not talk to your notes or to the empty air three feet above everyone's head. Look up frequently from your text and make contact with individual members of the audience.

I don't have to belabor the point that it is impossible to impress a person with your sincerity if you evade his eyes while talking to him. The same rule applies when you are speaking to an individual or to an audience of several hundred. Cultivate the habit of looking into as many faces as you can. Your audience will respond.

Too many speakers sound as though they have been wound up backstage, like some mechanical doll, and then sent out to deliver a prerecorded speech. Speaking stiffly is a very common fault and one that will inevitably result in a barrier between you and your listeners. At a party, even in a business situation, the animated speaker is the one who is given the attention. Whether it is an act or not, he gives the *impression* of being terribly interested and concerned by what he is saying. I know that a careful and deliberate style has certain advantages, but an audience will appreciate it if the speaker seems truly involved in his subject. An Olympian detachment may be perfectly suitable for a judge sitting in his courtroom but, as I observed earlier, a speech is not a dispassionate occasion. A good speech demands an emotional response, but you're not going to get it with a wooden delivery. Allow your natural enthusiasm for your subject to take over. Transmit a sense of excitement to those who have come to listen to you. Animation is a powerful asset in any speaker.

Audiences also appreciate tact. Unless you're speaking to a highly partisan crowd, it won't do to steamroller points of view that may differ from yours. It is a curious fact that most people tend to root for the underdog. If you sneer at the opposition and belittle everything they do, you may find that you will have lost sympathy for your own cause.

A corollary to that is to avoid sarcasm. A man who uses

sarcasm in his remarks gives the impression that he feels he is a superior person. Most audiences, at least in the United States, will react with a "who-does-he-think-he-is?" attitude, and if you try it you will have a very difficult time in getting them back on your side.

As in so many things, England provides a notable exception. There public sarcasm has been raised to an art, and a finely honed verbal insult is cherished. It has been a tradition in England's House of Parliament for centuries, but unless you plan to become an MP, don't cultivate it.

There is nothing more disconcerting for an audience than to listen to a man who appears to be uncomfortable on the platform. If you've ever gone to an amateur production or the performance of a school play, you probably have noticed an actor suffering from acute nervousness. He is ill at ease on the stage and very unsure of himself. The audience reacts by being uneasy *for him.* They are worried about his chances of blowing up in his lines or forgetting to make the right move at the right time. They pay so much attention to the hapless performer that they neglect the main action. I once attended a dinner which featured the inevitable speaker with coffee and dessert. After the usual introduction, our speaker of the evening rose ashen-faced and visibly trembling. He approached the microphone as though it were the guillotine and he the wretch about to be beheaded. The pleasant, warm buzz of conversation that had filled the room died suddenly. Everyone could see the poor fellow's plight. With bated breath we all agonized with him as he lurched perilously through his remarks. We all desperately wanted to see him safely through his ordeal because we felt no one should be allowed to suffer so. At the end, when he gratefully finished, the audience gave him what amounted to a standing ovation. He had made it after all, and we were proud of him. I don't think a person there could have provided a summary of the speech, but we cheered as wildly as if he had just delivered the sequel to the Gettysburg Address.

I suppose this is one way of insuring a good reception for your remarks, but you do it at peril to the communication of your ideas. An audience feels secure when it is in the hands of a poised and assured speaker. It will settle back and pay attention to what he is saying because it does not need to concern itself with the speaker's frame of mind. So practice poise in public. Even if butterflies are fluttering in your stomach, wear a mask of assurance.

But don't be too glib. Concentrate on what you are saying. It is worthwhile noting that nearly everyone who performs in public, whether it's an actor or a professional ball player, claims that the ability to concentrate is the difference between success and failure. A professional golfer brings his every faculty to bear on the shot he is about to make. Let his mind wander, for even a fraction of a second, and he misses the perfect stroke or fails to sink the crucial putt. Actors, particularly those appearing in a long-run hit, are especially prone to a wandering mind. They've read their lines so many times that it has become mechanical. As a result, their performance suffers.

Think about what you're saying as you say it. The sentence you are reading is not merely a collection of sounds. It is an idea expressed in a certain way, with certain shades of feeling. Concentrate on the meaning of your words, and think hard about the most effective way to communicate that meaning to your audience.

Your Appearance

Most speakers look awful on a platform. They may be well-groomed and dressed in the correct attire, but their posture is something any nine-year-old boy in dancing school would be ashamed of. Posture is more important than mere appearance. A speaker can actually stand in such a way that his posture interferes with his delivery. With shoulders drooping, chest concave, and knees bent, no speaker in the world can do more than gulp in a few shallow breaths of air. This means, of course, that he will soon run out and will be able to exercise little control over the breath he does have. Stand straight and tall when you're on a podium. Be conscious of your posture. Unbend your knees and throw your shoulders back. You should be planted firmly but lightly on the balls of your feet. You'll discover that correct posture will actually help you to relax.

But don't overcompensate. You're not a Marine drill sergeant. Keep your muscles loose and not locked in a stiff attitude of attention. I have seen speakers walk up to a microphone, snap to a position that can best be described as parade rest, and deliver a twenty-minute talk without moving an inch. It's a bit disconcerting because movement of some kind is expected from the speaker. It helps to reassure the audience that they are listening to someone who is alive.

Getting control over bodily movements is one of the most difficult things for public speakers to learn. Either they read through their speech motionless, or they insist on hopping around the platform. If you're using an amplification system, movement is always limited by the kind of microphone you use. If it's a neck microphone, you can wander all over the hall if you feel like it, with the length of cord the length of your tether. But if you're faced with a fixed desk microphone, you'd better stay close to it or your voice may fade and disappear in the middle of a sentence. Not that movement is impossible with a fixed microphone. Most of them are sensitive enough to pick up your voice from a reasonable range. But stay within that range. You can lean over the desk to make a point. You can turn to one side of the hall and then to the other. You can even step out from behind the podium as a change of pace. You can shrug your shoulders, throw up your arms, and nod your head if the urge strikes you. And it should strike you as you unveil your remarks. In private conversation, we don't sit and talk to each other like robots. We use the movement of our bodies to help us make our points. And so should all speakers.

But it is important to control movement. I remember once being entranced by a speaker who had a powerful and resonant voice. He seemed to be very much at ease on a platform and he was carried away by his subject matter—so much so that he emphasized his major points the way Elvis Presley used to put over a song in his earlier days.

"We cannot [rock] allow the situation to continue. We cannot [rock] allow the morals of our young people to be corrupted by these obscene books [rock], magazines [rock], and demeaning [rock], filthy [rock] films [rock]."

Instead of sharing his indignation at the spread of pornography in the community, his audience ended up by being slightly amused. His bumps and grinds would have done credit to any burlesque house, and indeed he seemed to be an animated advertisement for the sort of public wares he was condemning. He would have made his point more effectively had he exercised more control.

I would enjoy witnessing another performance like it, but I have never been so privileged. Another compulsive mover that I have seen only once was a smallish, worried-looking man who was warning his audience about the dangers of water pollution in a nearby river. The topic was an important one and affected all his listeners. But he dissipated his points by a curious habit he had of moving four or five steps to the left on one sentence, and then four or five steps to the right on the next. Watching him was like watching a tennis match. The trouble was, there was no net and no ball, and our eyes soon got tired moving back and forth.

These are extreme cases, I admit, but they serve the useful

purpose of emphasizing the need for you, as a speaker, to be aware of how you move your body and the importance of controlling it properly.

Facial expressions, too, can do grievous harm to the relationship between the speaker and his audience. In college, I audited a sociology course given by a professor who invariably lectured with his face set in a disapproving look, as though he smelled something faintly rotten in the room. I happened to know this man personally outside the classroom and recognized him as an unusually warm and generous human being. But I couldn't convince my fellow students. They all disliked him, although they grudgingly admitted he gave first-class lectures.

In the thirties there was a singer—I believe her name was Virginia O'Brien—who made quite a hit in the movies because of her unusual style of delivery. No matter what the lyrics, and they could be a passionate torch song or a finger-snapping up-beat tune, she sang with a perfect dead pan. Not a muscle would move in her face. For some reason people were intrigued and amused by this characteristic, and they flocked to see her. But not for long. She faded as quickly as she had bloomed because people soon tire of an expressionless face. This is equally true in the case of a public speaker.

Some speakers don't seem to realize it, but there is no law that says you can't smile at your audience. Or frown. Or look angry. Or express encouragement. In many cases a speaker is behind a raised lectern and perhaps all that an audience can see is his face. That face should be animated and alive, and not stare out like a dead fish.

When you rehearse your speech at home, practice it with facial expressions that emphasize and illustrate the points you are trying to make. Your performance will be much more effective if you do.

But What Do I Do with My Hands?

An acting coach once told me that he could spot a natural talent by the way an actor used his hands. For some reason public performers—and this includes speakers—don't seem to know what to do with their hands. They become gross, unwieldy objects unless they're called upon to perform some specific act like lighting a cigarette or pulling aside a window curtain.

Most speakers are lucky. They can grip the sides of the lectern and not look too awkward. But that position should be varied. If you're nervous, limit yourself to four basic positions: both hands on the lectern; right hand on the lectern, left hand down; reverse this position; and, finally, both hands at your sides. This will give sufficient variations so that the audience won't get the impression that you're locked, immobile, into place.

But really, hand movements are extremely effective, and you should practice them. Collections of famous speeches are available at your local library. Take a volume home and find a particularly eloquent oration. Then, in the privacy of your own bedroom, read it aloud in front of a mirror and let yourself go. Shake your fist at your imaginary audience, slice the air with wide sweeping motions. The first time through it will all seem rather exaggerated and foolish. But do it several more times, toning down your movements with each reading. Really think through what the passages mean and try to project yourself into the position of the historical figure who delivered this speech to an audience he sincerely wanted to motivate. If you have the imagination you'll begin to get the idea, and you'll start to use your hands, and indeed your entire body, to emphasize the points the speech is trying to make.

Because someone thought it important enough to put it

between the covers of a book, the speech you have been reading is probably one of those that changed the course of a nation or influenced the thoughts and behavior of people on a critical issue of the day. Your own speech may seem pitifully inadequate alongside it, being on the subject of how to improve debt equity ratios for centrally managed multinational corporations. However, now that you are in the swing of using your hands freely, try rehearsing your speech in the same way that you did the famous one. The points you are trying to make may not have the same wide-ranging significance, but you are trying to communicate certain ideas and points of view. You will discover, provided you concentrate on your rehearsal, that you are beginning to emphasize your arguments with a forceful and highly effective use of your hands. You may freeze a little once you're on the platform, but you've put down the groundwork for a better performance and at least some of your rehearsal will pay dividends when you're on your feet in public.

Your Voice

A man is judged by many of his characteristics, but among them his voice is one of the most important. Voices can soothe, irritate, intimidate, discourage, or inspire confidence. We have all encountered voices that grate on our nerves, and we instinctively try to avoid or tend to dislike people who produce such a sound. I am not talking about accents, patterns of speech, or regional dialects. I mean the physical sound that assaults our ears.

One of the most common irritants is the high-pitched voice. This comes about because the vocal cords are not relaxed. Listen to your own voice critically on a tape recorder, if you have one, and decide for yourself if your pitch is too high or thin. To correct this fault, consciously relax your vocal cords and force your voice down to a lower pitch. If you expect or hope to do much public speaking, you should practice these exercises regularly. In time they will become second nature.

Very often, these speakers who produce a thin sound also have the bad habit of speaking too fast: Their vocal cords are tense because most of the muscles of their body are equally tight. The result of this is a staccato, machine gun-like delivery. Speaking fast is perfectly all right as long as your audience can understand you. In some professions it is an asset. The men who do radio coverage of horse races generally spit out a torrent of words that rise in excitement and speed as the horses near the finish. They do this, I suppose, because their delivery is actually a reflection of what they are describing. But unless you plan to enter this somewhat specialized profession, moderation is the key word.

Another pair of faults that often go hand in hand are monotony and slowness of delivery. People react differently to tension and for some the response is to try to hold down the mounting pressure by speaking with a great deal of deliberation, keeping their voice as steady as they can. The result can drive an audience to distraction. We have all had the experience of listening to a speaker whose voice does not vary in its inflection, and who separates each word as if they were all precious jewels to be placed before us one by one. If you are in the habit of speaking fast, don't compensate by slowing your delivery to a crawl. Find a happy compromise between the two.

Change of Pace

A fully rounded and successful performance depends on variations. Don't be afraid to use a pause now and then. It can help emphasize a point you are trying to make. The phrase: "And why should we be concerned? Because the welfare of our children is at stake," needs a pause between the two sentences. Try reading them out loud without any sort of hesitation. And then insert a pause. You'll see the difference at once. In this case, a pause, properly used, not only heightens the dramatic effects of what you are trying to say, but it actually helps make the meaning clearer.

Now, read the same phrase again giving each word the same stress and the same emphasis. You will see that the message has not come through with sufficient force. Read it again, but this time stress the word *why*. Also stress the word *concerned,* but give it an upward inflection. You are, after all, asking a question. Read the first sentence fairly slowly. Then after you have made a pause, attack the word *because* and read the remainder of the sentence at a much faster pace and higher volume than the previous question.

What you have done, in one short passage, is to vary your pitch, volume, and tempo. You have given the passage new color and have provided it with a rhythm that speaks effectively to the ear. This is the process of putting together all the elements into a performance that exactly fits your subject matter and your personality. If you manage this throughout your entire speech, your presentation will be a memorable one, worthy of the effort you have invested in researching, writing, and delivering your remarks.

Part III

Through the Mill

Foreword

Those who have no patience with fiction are advised to skip this section. Congratulations. You have finished the book, and we thank you for your attention. However, others who are less disciplined may derive instruction from the following parable, which is an account of how an individual, named George Morris, was unexpectedly assigned the chore of delivering a speech before his local chamber of commerce. He was not given this task in recognition of any outstanding qualities of leadership or because he possessed a magnetic platform style. He was tapped because there were few in his company available that particular day, and those who were didn't particularly want to give the speech. In such unpredictable ways are heroes made.

As we follow George through his ordeal, we will see him grapple with the difficulty of zeroing in on a topic, developing a theme and thesis, doing his research, and preparing an outline. We shall share with George the agonies and ecstasies of composition as he patiently perfects a style of writing that will one day make him famous. We shall be silent eavesdroppers as George stammers through his first rehearsal, and applaud as he gains confidence. We shall accompany him as he

151

makes final preparations for his debut in public, and rejoice in his inevitable triumph.

We shall, in short, use the principles discussed earlier in this book as an object lesson in an imaginary real-life situation—one that never happened but one that could have developed exactly as it will now be described.

CHAPTER 9

The Ten-Minute Ordeal
of George Morris

I

Once upon a time there lived a man of few faults and indifferent virtue who had fashioned for himself a comfortable
life in a comfortable town. Industrious, conscientious, and
not especially forceful, George Morris occupied the position
of a section head in the budget department of the Acme
Lighting Fixture Company, Inc., a manufacturing firm whose
business was the fabrication of commercial outdoor lighting fixtures used by shopping centers and municipalities
to turn night into day. George's qualities had not escaped the
attention of his superiors who were able, quite rightly, to dismiss him almost entirely from their minds. His fellow employees also thought highly of George. He represented no
threat to their ambitions. Although one of three section
heads in the budget department, it was generally understood
that he would not succeed to the position of department

manager upon the imminent retirement of Andrew "Dandy Andy" Durland. There was some doubt that Oscar Anderson, financial vice-president of Acme Lighting Fixture, even knew who George was, and so it was unlikely he would elevate him to a post of such authority.

It became evident one recent Monday morning, however, that Oscar Anderson was indeed aware of George's existence. The emissary who carried this news was none other than Dandy Andy Durland who appeared unannounced in the doorway of George's cubicle, his white hair carefully brushed, his pink cheeks glistening, and the blue cornflower that had become his trademark firmly anchored in the buttonhole of his jacket. George looked up and waited for the greeting that invariably opened their conversations.

"Morning, George. Keeping you busy?"

Without even thinking, George shot back the ritual reply. "Plugging away, Andy. Plugging away."

"Attaboy." Durland settled into the visitor's chair and got down to business. "Listen, George, I've just been in to see the Big O and he wants you to do a job for him." The Big O was, of course, Oscar Anderson, and directives never came from him. It was always Durland who assigned the tasks. George thought that this had to be something special, and he was right.

"You see," Durland went on, "there's this chamber of commerce luncheon next month and they've invited three of the industries around town to make presentations of what they do. We're one of them, so we have to send a speaker, and Anderson wants you to do it."

George stared at Durland blankly. "Do what?" he said.

"Do the presentation."

"Write it you mean?"

"Write it and give it."

George began to feel the first flush of the panic that was to become so familiar to him in the weeks ahead. "Why me?" he asked with a puzzled look on his face.

"Well, it's the week of the sales conference in Chicago and all the brass will be gone. Anderson would do it himself but he's got something on that day. He and I talked it over and decided that you knew Acme about as well as anybody in the company and could do a great job." As Durland got up to leave, George felt like grabbing his sleeve. "Don't worry about it, George. They only want a ten-minute talk. You can do it in your sleep." Durland moved to the door.

"But what do I talk about?" A note of desperation had crept into George's voice.

"About Acme Lighting Fixture. See you later." And Durland was gone.

George leaned back in his chair to consider the situation. He had never before appeared in public. No, that wasn't quite right. In the eighth grade he was one of the pirates in *The Pirates of Penzance*, but that wasn't the same thing. As a member of the chorus he was just one of a dozen kids on the stage. But at the luncheon he would be standing alone in front of perhaps several hundred of the most prominent businessmen in town. There was that feeling of panic again, but this time it hit him in the pit of his stomach. Resolutely, he put the scene out of his mind.

Then it suddenly occurred to him that this was an honor, and an opportunity. Out of all the available employees, they had picked him. He decided to telephone his wife. Fortunately, she was home.

"Hello, Marge. Guess what happened?"

"Andy Durland wore a Venus flytrap in his buttonhole this morning and it bit him in the face."

"Come on, Marge. This is serious. I'm going to make a speech."

"Okay, go ahead."

"No, not now. Next month at the chamber of commerce luncheon. Oscar Anderson asked me to do it."

"No kidding. What about?"

"About the company."

"You going to tell them the truth?"

"How do you mean?"

"About it being a crummy joint where you've been spinning your wheels for the last twelve years and haven't had a decent raise in four."

"Sure, that's a great idea."

"Well, what are you going to tell them?"

"I'll think of something."

"Okay, Tiger. Regular time?"

"Yeah, regular time."

George hung up the phone feeling suddenly depressed. Marge had a point. What *was* he going to talk about? George reached for a pad of paper and began nibbling at the end of a pencil. Then he wrote:

Good afternoon, ladies and gentlemen, and thank you. As you know, I'm here as a representative of the Acme Lighting Fixture Company, and I've come to tell you a little about who we are and what we do. Acme was established in 1925 in this town and our headquarters have been here ever since. The company provides employment for 485 people and therefore contributes substantially to the economic prosperity of our community. Our principal business has always been lighting fixtures. For example, we make poles used by cities to light their streets. Until recently these were made of steel. But today most of them are made of an aluminum alloy and are designed to break away at the impact of a car. This is a major advance and an important safety feature that has already saved the lives of an estimated. . . .

George had the feeling that something was wrong, and he paused to review his efforts. He started from the top.

"Good afternoon, ladies and gentlemen." Would ladies be present, or would it be an exclusively male audience? "And thank you." Who was he thanking? And what was he thanking them for? He made a note to find out who would be introducing him. Now, what had he told them so far? Being a methodical man, George compiled a list:

1. Acme's contribution to the community.
2. Changes in manufacturing over the years.
3. Safety as an important consideration in street lighting.

It struck him he was telling his audience too many different things all at once. Shouldn't his speech have a single, central idea? He rather thought it should. Then his eye caught the phrase about how Acme "contributes substantially to the economic prosperity of our community." That word "substantially" bothered him. It was so vague. He made another note to himself. By this time he decided he needed to know the following:

1. Who would be in the audience?
2. Who would be introducing him?
3. What was the central issue of the speech?
4. What was the exact size of Acme's annual payroll?

And finally, as an afterthought:

5. How did Acme's payroll compare with others in town?

George thought the best place to find the answers to his first two questions would be from the chamber of commerce. He had had no contacts within the chamber himself, but he was sure that there had to be correspondence between the chamber of commerce and the company. Probably Oscar Anderson's secretary had it. He reached for the phone to ask

Myrtle if she knew the name of the man who had issued the invitation to the luncheon.

II

Mr. Lasker from the chamber of commerce had been very helpful. Mr. Lasker was the president of the second largest bank in town, but he also was program chairman for the chamber of commerce luncheon. At first George was somewhat hesitant about telephoning such a prominent citizen, but he could see no alternative. When George finally got through to the bank he wasn't a bit surprised to discover that Mr. Lasker was protected by a most efficient secretary who demanded to know George's business before she agreed to connect him. When he explained the reason for his call her stiffness vanished and George found himself talking to Mr. Lasker, who assured him that he could have all the time he wanted and was happy to answer any questions he might have.

"A damn good idea," Mr. Lasker had said. "I always make it a point myself to get a feel for the audience before I start on any speech I have to give. I wish more of our speakers would take the trouble, and, by the way, please call me Ed."

And so it was on the familiar basis of George and Ed that they discussed the forthcoming luncheon. The audience would be mostly businessmen but a few were expected to bring their wives. George would be introduced by Mr. Benson, the president of the chamber, and he would be the last of the three speakers. The others on the program included a Mr. Zaynes, who owned the largest automobile dealership in town, and a Mr. De Silva, who ran a contracting firm that frequently did road construction.

Ed Lasker told George that these industry presentation luncheons sponsored by the chamber were a good idea, but that most speakers made the mistake of simply describing their business "as if they were reading from a prospectus." He said the audience always appreciated it if the speaker could talk about the enterprise he was representing in a livelier way, by relating it more closely to the community. As he put it, "It's not so much what the business is, it's more what the business means that interests our people."

On the cafeteria line that noon George was thinking about what Ed Lasker had told him, when his good friend, Henry Paul from traffic, caught up with him.

"Hey, George," Henry said. "I hear you're going to make a speech." George admitted that this was so. "What's it going to be about?" Henry asked.

"That's just what Ed Lasker and I were talking about before I came down to lunch," George said as they took their seats.

"Ed Lasker?" Henry looked properly impressed. "You mean Edward J. Lasker, president of the First Union Bank?"

"Yep," George said, as he broke open a cellophane envelope of crackers. "He's the program chairman for the luncheon. He thought I ought to tie my description of the company into the life of the community."

"Hey, you lost me," Henry said. "Take it from the top." Quickly, George reviewed the events of the morning, summarizing his conversation with the banker. Henry Paul listened attentively and nodded occasionally.

"That's kind of tough," Henry said at last. "I mean, you know, we make light poles and stuff. Nothing very sexy about that."

"I know," George agreed gloomily.

"On the other hand," Henry went on, "my kid came home from school the other night and told me about a movie he had seen that day. It was all about artificial light and what it meant to the growth of cities. Now he's got to write a paper on the subject."

"Where's he getting his information?"

"The library, where else? Listen, you want me to get you the name of that film, I will. It was put out by some big electric company."

"Thanks, I'd appreciate it. Maybe I ought to go to the library myself. They're open till seven on Mondays, aren't they?"

"Yeah."

The two friends ate silently. At last Henry looked at George with an admiring grin. "So it's Ed and George, eh? Not bad, buddy. Not bad."

George smiled. "When you want that second mortgage, let me know. I'll talk to Ed about it."

III

The library was nearly deserted when George arrived there shortly before six that evening. The public library was unfamiliar territory to George. He had been in the building perhaps two or three times before and he wasn't sure where to go. But he spotted a desk with an "information" sign on it and decided to start there.

"Good evening." The pleasant-looking girl behind the desk nodded helpfully. "I wonder if you could help me?"

"I'll try." A smaller sign, also on the desk, identified the girl as Miss Waverly.

"I'm with the Acme Lighting Fixture Company," George started, "and I'm interested in. . . ."

"Oh, I'm sorry," Miss Waverly interrupted, "but you'll have to come tomorrow. The man who handles our purchases leaves at five."

"Oh, I'm not trying to sell anything," George protested. "I've come to get some information because I've got to give a speech."

Miss Waverly's face softened. "I see," she said. "What about?"

There was that question again. Every time he told anyone about the speech they invariably asked what it was going to be about. George sketched in the details for Miss Waverly. "So you see," he concluded, "what I'm after is some material on artificial light."

Miss Waverly looked thoughtful. "You don't mean how it's produced? You don't want any technical literature?" George agreed that, no, he did not want any technical literature. Miss Waverly pressed on. "Are you interested primarily in interior lighting? Special effects?"

George wasn't sure.

"The uses of lighting?"

"Maybe."

"Lighting in schools, airports, public buildings?"

George nodded. "That's more like it."

"I think we could get you some material on the extent and use and perhaps even some statistics on costs, if that would be helpful."

"I just don't know."

Miss Waverly decided to try a different approach. "I'll tell you what, Mr. . . . ."

"Morris. George Morris."

"I'll tell you what, Mr. Morris. Why don't you spend a few minutes over in our reference department. Just browse around and maybe it will give you some ideas. Here, let me show you what we have." Miss Waverly stood and led the way to a corner of the main reading room. For the next half hour George and Miss Waverly consulted several encyclopedias—under the general heading of lighting they found specific citations in five categories that included airports, artificial, public utilities, schools, and stores. In the *Reader's Guide to Periodical Literature* they discovered a reference to an article on outdoor lighting that appeared in a publication called *The American City*. Miss Waverly produced a copy of the magazine and George jotted down the address of its editorial offices. In the main card catalog George and Miss Waverly uncovered an entire library on the subject of lighting, artificial and otherwise, and George noted those he felt might be helpful.

At the end of their search George had to agree there was more than enough research material available for his speech. His only problem was going to be to narrow it down so that he knew what to look for.

"Think about it," Miss Waverly advised him. "Put down some rough notes. Begin to focus in on some aspect of this subject—something that you're interested in and something you think your audience is going to appreciate. Then we can take it from there."

George was in the middle of thanking Miss Waverly for her efforts when he noticed the time. Nearly a quarter of seven, and he had forgotten to telephone Marge to say he'd be late.

IV

All things considered, the dinner went pretty well. The roast, of course, was overcooked and Marge, while she wasn't at her friendliest, wasn't downright hostile either. After George had prostrated himself on the living room floor in apology for his thoughtlessness, Marge decided to reopen relations with him, at least to the extent of talking to him about his problem.

"It seems to me," she said as they relaxed over coffee, "that you've got a choice to make. Either you tell them about Acme Lighting Fixture or you talk about artificial illumination. You can't do both in ten minutes."

"No, I don't agree," George said. "The whole idea of the lunch is to describe the various industries in this town."

"But what about that thing Mr. Lasker said to you. Didn't

he say that they were more interested in what the businesses meant than what they did?"

"That's right," George agreed. "But I can't give them a lecture on the development of artificial light from Edison to the present. What I've got to do is put them together."

"In ten minutes?" Marge looked doubtful.

"Look, I can do a quick thumbnail sketch of the history of Acme. Let's say that takes two or three minutes. Then I can tell them what all this means to the economy of the town. In terms of dollars spent here, homes built, and so forth. Another two minutes. That leaves five minutes."

"My mathematical genius."

George went right on. "And that's when I talk about what the industry means to people. How it's affected their lives."

"What are you going to tell them?"

George stared gloomily at his coffee cup. "That's the problem," he said. "I don't know."

"Well," Marge said thoughtfully, "let's start from the beginning. Suppose artificial light had never been invented. How would our lives be different? What can we do that people living two hundred years ago couldn't do?"

"For one thing," George said, "people can be more active for a longer period of time. In the old days, when darkness came all they had were candles and torches."

"Yes," Marge interrupted, "and only the rich could afford enough candles to make a really bright light."

"And so most people simply went to bed when the sun set. Think of the man-hours that wasted. Artificial light extended the working day. It made society more productive."

"I don't know if that was such a hot idea," Marge said.

"Well, it's given us more time to play, too. For instance, look at Bobby." Bobby was their thirteen-year-old son.

"What about Bobby?" Marge asked.

"He's out playing softball. Under lights." George got up

and began to pace the room. "You know, Marge, I think we've got something. I think we can say that our entire lives and our entire way of living have been changed because of the industry that's represented by Acme Lighting Fixture. How about that?"

"You're going to have to back that statement up," Marge pointed out.

"I know it," George said. "But I've got a few leads. Miss Waverly was very helpful."

"Miss who?" Marge's voice had taken on a curiously remote quality.

"The librarian," George explained. "You know . . . at the library."

"That's where they're usually found."

"Oh come on, Marge. It was all business. Anyway, I'm going to make some notes while the idea is still fresh and then write some letters. I ought to be done by ten-thirty or so. I'll meet you at the eleven o'clock news."

"Maybe Miss Waverly will be on it," Marge said.

George grinned at her, gathered up his papers, and went down to the basement where a small corner off the recreation room had been set aside for his "study." He switched on his desk lamp, took a pad of yellow paper from his drawer, and began to lecture to himself.

"Miss Waverly is absolutely right. I've got to decide on an approach, pick a focus. And then she can help. I didn't know librarians had such nice legs. Well, what about the idea Marge and I were talking over? Let me see, how did I put it?" George wrote the following lines on his note pad:

Our society has been fundamentally changed by the introduction and widespread use of artificial illumination.

George didn't know it, but he had just written the thesis of his speech. He did wonder, however, if he could substantiate that statement. Perhaps some of the sources he had uncovered could give him a lead. On a separate piece of paper he made another list:

1. *The American City* (a publication)
2. Edison Electric Institute (a trade association of public utilities)
3. Street and Highway Safety Lighting Bureau

He then wrote down the names of all the major electric companies and the principal utilities in the country. The list was surprisingly lengthy and it consisted of the names of organizations he and Miss Waverly had found that afternoon. George next turned to serious composition and wrote the following letter:

> I am currently engaged in a research project which has led me into the general area of adequate street illumination. I am interested particularly in trying to measure the contribution of artificial light to the growth and development of cities, both historically and at present.
>
> I would appreciate receiving any material that you publish relating to this subject. Or perhaps you could direct me to a source where I might find it.
>
> Thank you for your help.
>
> Sincerely,
George R. Morris

This same letter would go to the public relations departments of all the organizations on his list. One of the pool secretaries could type them in the morning. After all, it *was* company business.

George's next move was to compile still another list. This one consisted of the topics he intended to cover in his speech. It read like this:

1. Opening.
2. Brief history of the company.

a. Get anecdotes from Harry Albright, foreman, day shift. Harry with company thirty-seven years.

b. Check secretary's office. Sec'y-treas. must have historical material.

3. What the company means to the community.

a. Taxes.

b. Payroll.

c. Civic involvement.

d. Individual employee involvement.

4. The industry behind the company. Lighting fixtures more than just business that provides employment and benefits town. Artificial light benefit to society as a whole.

a. Extends work; society more productive.

b. More play.

c. Lighting in:

a. schools;

b. hospitals;

c. airports.

d. Safety.

5. Conclusions: We take artificial illumination for granted, but would literally be in the dark ages without it. This the real significance and contribution of Acme Lighting Fixture.

6. Close.

George put this document in a safe place. He didn't know it but he had just written the initial outline for his speech. He recognized that these notes gave him a sense of direction, and he was aware that he had a lot of thinking to do. Certainly, he'd have to go back to the library again. But Marge would understand. Thinking about Miss Waverly, George switched off his study light and headed upstairs to join Marge and the eleven o'clock news.

V

It was close to four o'clock when George returned to his office. It had been a most productive day. Arthur Allers, secretary and treasurer of Acme Lighting, couldn't have been more cooperative. He had turned over the company's historical file and had even helped George locate the material he needed. After spending an hour and a half on the project, Allers paid George a compliment.

"You're a thorough man, George. I'll say that for you."

"This is my first time out," George explained. "I've never given a speech before so I'm not really sure how much stuff I'm going to need."

"Listen," Allers said, as he escorted George to the door of his office. "I hadn't planned to go to that luncheon, but do you mind if I show up? I'll be interested to see how it all comes out."

"Sure thing, Art. And many thanks for all your help."

As George walked down the hall, he reflected that being on a first-name basis with an officer of the company and a member of the board of directors wasn't a bad development in his career with Acme.

In the next hour, George had spent some time with the payroll department and then the tax people. They had been equally helpful with information. After lunch, he had paid a call on Harry Albright, the man who had been an employee of the company for thirty-seven years. As George had expected, Harry was full of anecdotes about Acme's early history. With his years of service, Harry was a sort of privileged character. He called all the brass by their first names and seemed to know everything about them. Acme was Harry's entire life and he was perfectly willing to talk about it for hours. This is exactly what he had done that afternoon, and

George had a full notebook when he finally managed to tear himself away.

George recognized that his job now was to select, edit, and put his information together in an orderly fashion. He sat down at his desk and pulled a note pad closer. After only two days on the project, reaching for a note pad had already become almost second nature to George. But before he could start to put his thoughts in order, Andy Durland made an unexpected appearance in his office.

"Hello, George. Keeping you busy?" Andy sounded rushed.

"Plugging away, Andy," George replied mechanically, wondering why Andy looked a little irritated. "Plugging away."

"I ran into Oscar Anderson a little while ago," Andy began. "He said he'd gotten a couple of calls about you."

"Oh?"

"Mr. Lasker of the First Union Bank called to say you'd been in touch with him. He said some nice things about you."

George nodded.

"And then Art Allers said you'd spent some time with him this morning. He told Anderson he thought you were going about it the right way."

"That's nice to hear," George said.

"Yeah. Yeah, that's right." Andy edged to the door, looking troubled. "Anything I can do to help, you let me know, huh?"

"Sure," George said. "I sure will. And thanks."

"Anything at all, now. Oscar told me to give you all the help you needed."

"That's very nice of you, Andy," George said. "I'll remember that."

"Okay," Andy said. "See you around."

After Andy's exit George smiled slightly to himself. Andy Durland was unused to anyone on his staff making a name for himself. Whenever it happened Andy always got nervous. George decided to forget about Durland and settled down to business.

Should he try another outline? George decided against it. What he did instead was to reduce each piece of information he had gathered that day into a few succinct, separate phrases. He decided he would not worry about their proper order at this time. But perhaps that evening he could put them together in some sensible sequence. For the moment, these would be his building blocks—the elements of his outline.

It was a little after five when he finished. As he stuffed his papers in his briefcase, George considered the advisability of another call on Miss Waverly. But he shook his head. Two evenings in a row would be stretching it just a bit. He'd talk over the day's events with Marge and spend a little time that night in his study. George snapped out the light and headed for the parking lot.

VI

As he had promised himself, George spent most of the evening talking his speech over with Marge. He did this again the next night. And the one following that. During the day he discussed ideas with his colleagues. So relentless was he in pursuit of their opinions over the next few days that people began to avoid him in the halls and the company cafeteria. It was Marge who finally brought him up short.

"I am sick and tired of that damn speech," she told him one night.

"How do you think I feel about it?" George snapped back irritably. "I've had it up to here with the thing. What do I know about writing a speech anyway? Or giving one? They shouldn't have done it to me in the first place. It's not right. It's unfair."

"Don't whine, George," she said. "You sound just like Bobby throwing a tantrum." George shut up and sulked in his chair. "What about all that literature you've been getting? Isn't it any help?"

"Oh sure," George admitted. "I've gotten all sorts of booklets and reprints from the utilities and electric companies. But the trouble is, they're full of facts. I've got more facts than I know what to do with. My problem is trying to find a focus . . . something to hang the whole thing on. Something to give it some life and some relevancy, and not just a recitation."

"Well, try and forget about it tonight," Marge advised him. "Relax and don't force it. Maybe it'll just come."

George recognized that her advice was sound, but through the entire evening the speech was always in his mind. Even after they had gone to bed that night he persisted in thinking about it.

He lay on his back, arms folded behind his head, staring up at the patterns the street lamp outside made on the ceiling. Beside him, Marge began to breathe evenly. She was asleep. The night sounds began crowding in on George. Somewhere on the block a car door slammed shut. The sound of footsteps, and a woman's laugh. In the distance a dog barked. And then George heard the urgent sound of an ambulance siren. It made him think of the time that Bobby had to be rushed to the hospital in the middle of the night because of a ruptured appendix. Help had come within minutes, and Bobby was out of the operating room within two hours of the first call for help.

George tried to imagine what that moment would have been like if it hadn't been for light. The ambulance was able to travel swiftly through well-lighted streets. There was no need for the driver to grope his way. And he had no trouble in finding their house, either. George and Marge had all the lights on. After the lightning-fast trip to the hospital, George recalled the brightly lit emergency room where an examination quickly confirmed the need for an immediate operation. He remembered how the staff reacted like a well-drilled team. There was no hesitation and no fumbling. He wondered if they would have moved as quickly and efficiently with only candles or torches to guide them. And the idea of operating by candlelight was simply unthinkable. No, his thesis was certainly sound in that instance. Adequate lighting may have made the difference between life and death in Bobby's case. It was a very real and concrete example, and one that had been repeated many times in the town.

Repeated many times in the town! Not what light meant to any community. What it meant to his community, to the town of Phillipsburg, Iowa. That was it! If he could find some real anecdotes relating to the life of the town his audience would be bound to react. Instead of talking abstractly he'd be making it very immediate for everyone in the room.

George sat up in bed and gave Marge's backside an exuberant slap. "I've got it," he yelped.

Marge shot bolt upright. "What . . . what . . . what?" was all she could manage.

"The focus for the speech," George announced triumphantly.

Marge was still struggling with the cobwebs of sleep, but she looked dangerous. Then suddenly the fire in her eyes changed to a laugh. "You big . . . ," she was trying to find the exact word. "Nut," she said at last. "Is that all you woke me up for?"

It suddenly occurred to George that Marge was a very attractive woman. He pulled her down beside him on the pillow. "No," he said, running his hand over her warm bare shoulder. "No, that's not the only reason."

As he held Marge closer, Miss Waverly's face unexpectedly appeared in his mind. George was surprised at his own behavior. "To hell with Miss Waverly," George said to himself. "To absolute hell with her." In another moment, he had forgotten all about Miss Waverly.

VII

The following night, immediately after dinner, George got down to the serious business of constructing an outline. Working slowly and carefully, he put each piece of the jigsaw puzzle into its proper place:

1. Opening. (He'd think about that later.)
2. Start off by saying that assignment is to describe my company. But the true meaning of any business is not found only in a simple description of its operations. True meaning is best discovered through its relationship to the community that surrounds it.
3. In the case of this town and Acme Lighting Fixture Company, the relationship is long and mutually beneficial.
4. In fact, it is fair to say that, without the support of Phillipsburg, Acme would not be in existence. On the other hand, without the products manufactured by the industry Acme represents, life in our community would be very different from the one we know. (George recognized this as a restatement of his central theme, and he knew instinctively that it was important for him to set it forth early in the speech.)
5. And so, what I am going to tell you this afternoon is the story of a company and a community.
6. It starts in the year 1925 when a young metalworker became ambitious enough to branch out on his own. Borrowing $2,000 from his brother-in-law, this young man, who was named Ira Tapton, opened a small shop to manufacture lighting fixtures to be sold to municipalities. He saw that more and more towns were putting in electric street lamps, and he felt there was an opportunity in this field.

7. He didn't have to look far to prove he was right. His own hometown of Phillipsburg was about to install electric street lighting and was asking for bids. Tapton submitted one and won. So from the very beginning, the community supported him.

8. Business prospered until the depression. Municipalities everywhere were cutting back on expenditures, and appropriations for street lighting fixtures were nonexistent. Business considerations dictated that Tapton should get rid of some of his employees.

9. Instead, Tapton called a meeting of all his men and gave them a clear picture of conditions. He said he was not going to fire a single one of them if he could help it. All agreed to reduced pay, and even Tapton voluntarily limited his own take from the business to the pay level of his foremen. (George got this anecdote from Harry Albright.)

10. Finally when Tapton's back was to the wall, the community again came to the rescue. This time it was in the form of a line of credit granted by the First Union Bank—Edward J. Lasker's bank.

11. This helped tide Acme over. During World War II, Acme subcontracted for military work and diversified. This diversification resulted in other markets besides municipal street lighting requirements and after the war Acme began a period of growth that has still not stopped.

12. Acme has repaid its debt to the community in many ways. Document this:

a. Amount of annual payroll ($4 million). The purchasing power this represents is spent largely in Phillipsburg.
b. Local taxes paid by company.
c. Community affairs in which company is active.

13. In addition, individual employees contribute.

a. Most own homes in the town and pay local taxes.

b. Deeply involved in the political life of the town. Cite examples of Acme employees who have held or hold public office.

c. Cite examples of employees who have contributed time and money to charities, hospitals, etc. Get unusual examples of individual service.

14. Transition here. But dollars spent and hours freely given are not the full extent of Acme's contribution to Phillipsburg and towns like it all over the country. But towns are made up of people, so let's talk about three of them.

15. Get anecdote illustrating how adequate lighting in public places saved a human life. Use Bobby as an example if none other available.

16. Get another story of how a young person managed to get a college education by studying nights. It would have been difficult, if not impossible, without artificial illumination.

17. Get story of how a man rose to become a business success because he was able to keep enterprise open at nights. There was not enough business during the day for him to turn the corner. But an added four hours a night made the difference.

18. Go from these three specific cases to the general observation of what the warmth of light means to us in terms of safety, convenience, opportunities that could never have existed without artificial illumination.

19. Conclude that this is Acme's real role . . . a contribution to making life richer, fuller, and more agreeable for all of us.

George looked over the outline and was satisfied. He would show it to Marge when he came home from work the next day. If she approved, he would start writing it then.

VIII

As it happened, Marge did approve. They had gone over the outline together and Marge had asked some questions that forced George to become more precise in his thinking in a few key areas. But generally, both agreed that the outline passed inspection and that it was okay for George to start writing.

George pulled off the cover of the battered old portable he had owned ever since college and sat down confidently. As he inserted a piece of paper into the machine, he thought to himself, "I am now going to write this speech."

The net effect of that thought was exactly as if someone had tied his hands behind his back. For a full five minutes George stared at the paper in his typewriter without making a move toward the keyboard. He had frozen, dried up completely.

"This is ridiculous," he said to himself. "You've got to start somewhere, so write something. Anything."

Forcing his fingers to the keys, George wrote:

Good evening, ladies and gentlemen, and . . . .

What was he doing! It was a luncheon affair. And what was the name of the man who was going to introduce him? Also the names of his fellow-panelists? George searched through his notes and started over:

Good afternoon, ladies and gentlemen. And thank you Mr. Benson, Mr. Zaynes, and Mr. De Silva . . . .

No, no, no! It was all right to thank Mr. Benson for introducing him, but why was he thanking the other two? They hadn't done anything except speak before he did. George felt the need of an anecdote, a story to start things off. But what was so funny about a light pole? Maybe a dog found a light pole interesting, but he couldn't think of anything else that might. Hey . . . not a bad idea. George attacked the typewriter again:

> Good afternoon, ladies and gentlemen, and thank you, Mr. Benson. Mr. Zaynes and Mr. De Silva have both given us interesting accounts of their businesses. This puts me at a disadvantage, because I'm in the light pole business, and about the only thing that finds us interesting is a dog.

George read it over and smiled to himself. Not bad. Not bad at all. He decided to run upstairs and read his joke to Marge.

"Ugh!" was her reaction.

George's face fell. "You don't like it?" he asked.

"It's about as appealing as a wet diaper," was her comment.

"But a speech is supposed to start out with a joke," George pointed out.

"So write one," Marge said.

George crept back down to his study and stared at his handiwork. All right, maybe it wasn't so funny. But what could he say? He wondered if Zaynes and De Silva were finding their speeches equally difficult. The three stooges, he thought to himself. A car dealer, a guy who does contracting for the roads, and me, a guy in the. . . . Struck by a sudden idea, George made his fourth attempt:

> Good afternoon, ladies and gentlemen, and thank you, Mr. Benson. I think your program chairman, Mr. Lasker, has put together a most interesting package for this meeting. We have heard from Mr. Zaynes about cars and from Mr. De Silva about roads. It is now my turn to talk to you about a business that makes it possible for Mr. Zaynes' cars to run on Mr. De Silva's roads after the

sun goes down. With all due modesty, the Acme Lighting Fixture Company's job is to shed some light on the activities that have just been described to us.

That didn't feel too bad. He decided to press on. But how was he going to get from his opening statement to the first principal point in his outline? Making the transition wasn't going to be easy. He considered and then discarded the notion of moving in directly with something like, "I am going to describe for you the history, progress, and current situation of my company." That was too abrupt. Instead, he wrote:

Of course, helping to shed light on the activities of this town is something that my company has been doing since 1925. I suppose I could enumerate the vehicular lighting fixtures we have supplied to Phillipsburg over the years. Somewhere in our records I am sure there is an accounting of how many commercial specialty fixtures we have supplied to our town's educational institutions, hospitals, libraries, and mercantile centers. But this would miss the point. This would not begin to describe the Acme Lighting Fixture Company, for it would not describe the unique relationship that exists between this community of ours and the company I represent.

Very neat, George thought to himself. But why all the five-dollar words? I don't talk like that, he told himself, so why should I write that way? And so, "I suppose I could enumerate the vehicular lighting fixtures we have supplied," became, "I suppose I could list all the light poles we have supplied." Similarly, "educational institutions" became "schools" and "mercantile centers" was transformed into "shopping centers." That made it, in George's opinion, neater, simpler, and more direct. And he was right. George continued:

Our relationship has been so close that I think it is fair to say that, without the support of Phillipsburg, Acme would not be in existence today. On the other hand, without the products manufactured by Acme, life in our town would be very different from the one we have become used to.

Wait a minute. The image of Miss Hazleton, his fifth-grade teacher, flashed unexpectedly through George's mind. She was the one who had this thing about prepositions. She'd fly into a rage if you ended a sentence with one. George read over the sentence he had just completed, and sure enough, there it was. "To hell with it," George thought to himself. "Miss Hazleton's not going to be in the audience." He moved ahead:

> And so, what I'm going to tell you this afternoon is the story of a company and a community, and how each has had a profound effect on the other.

The next section of the speech went remarkably well. He merely followed his detailed outline and was pleasantly surprised to find he could practically copy it down, word for word. He hadn't realized, when he was preparing his outline, that he was virtually doing a finished version of the speech. It was an unexpected bonus. Within a matter of hours he had written more than three full pages and had reached the transitional point in the speech where he would begin to use the anecdotal material concerning three individuals. It was a good place to stop for the night.

IX

For three full days George never once glanced at the speech. Instead, he searched for and eventually discovered the anecdotal material he needed. Because of this forced separation from his creative efforts, he was able, on the fourth night, to take a hard objective look at what he had written. He was pleased with most of it. But there were places where he was able to tighten his own prose and, by substituting one word for another, he found he could make it read better.

For example, in the section where he was describing Ira Tapton's first contract, he had written, "Ira Tapton took swift advantage of the opportunity." George changed this to read, "Ira Tapton leaped at the chance." This simple change made the whole sentence seem more alive. In another paragraph, describing the effects of the depression, George had said, "Business slowed and, after a few erratic starts, virtually disappeared." Instead, he substituted, "Business sputtered erratically for a while, and then died almost completely." It was remarkable, he reflected, how dramatically a verb change could alter a sentence.

George now addressed himself to the transition. He had ended his work the other night with this paragraph:

This list of Acme employees who have given freely of their time and energy to community activities is long and varied. It ranges from Bertha McCloud in our accounting department, who sets aside three nights a week to act as a nurse's helper at Memorial Clinic, to George Binder, one of our shift foremen who uses his vacation each year to take six youngsters up to his farm. The youngsters are referred to George by our juvenile court. For some it has meant a glimpse of a new way of life and, perhaps, even an opportunity for that new life.

Being an old hand at writing transitions, George had no trouble in leading into his next thought:

Yes, the company and its people have meant a chance at life for many of our fellow citizens. Perhaps it meant the difference between life and death for one little boy who woke up in the middle of the night . . . .

And George was off and running with the story of what happened to Bobby that night he and Marge called the hospital. He wrote it vividly and simply because the memory of that experience was still fresh in his mind.

Carried on by his own momentum, he suddenly found himself at the wrap-up of his speech. He knew instinctively that here was where he should make his climax and then bow out gracefully. Feeling a little anxious, he began:

> And so you can see what light has meant to the community, and what the community has meant to Acme Lighting Fixture Company. Thank you.

George looked it over and shook his head. "Boy," he said to himself, "that sure stinks. Get a grip on yourself and try it again."

> For John Unger, the opportunity to keep his store open at night was the key to success. For Charlotte Bivens, the lights in her classrooms and library meant an opportunity she could never have had in a darker time. And for Bobby Morris—my own son—it meant life itself. These are but three people in our town. But for all of us, the warmth of light means safety, convenience, and opportunity. This is Acme's real role. It is the contribution we can make in helping to realize a richer, fuller, and more agreeable life. And we, in turn, can never forget that this community made it possible for us to make such a contribution. Thank you.

It was finished at last. George could hardly believe it. The speech that had seemed such a monster two weeks ago had been tamed. He had wrestled with it and managed to pin it down on six and a half pages of manuscript paper. Sure, he would make changes, but the worst part was over. He could hardly wait to read it aloud to Marge.

X

"Stand up straight," Marge said. "And hold your shoulders back." George snapped to attention. "George, you're not at West Point," Marge went on. "Stand straight but relax. That's better. Okay, go ahead."

George cleared his throat and began. "Good afternoon, ladies and gentlemen, and thank you, Mr. Ben. . . ."

"Just a minute," Marge interrupted. "Shouldn't we rig a lectern of some kind? After all, you'll be speaking from one, won't you?"

"I don't know," George confessed.

"Well, hadn't you better find out?"

George nodded. "I'll ask."

"What about a microphone?"

"I'll ask."

"Maybe you'll just get up and speak from your place."

"I'll ask. Now, can we start?"

"Okay . . . And now for our next speaker, it gives me great pleasure to introduce the most marvelous man in the world, George Morris."

"Marge, come on!"

"Well, I think you are."

George gave Marge one of his whatever-am-I-going-to-do-with-you looks and took it from the top.

"Good afternoon, ladies and gentlemen, and thank you, Mr. Benson. I think your program chairman, Mr. Lasker, has put together a most interesting package for this meeting. . . ."

"No," Marge cut in. "You don't think it's interesting at all."

George frowned at her. "What does that have to do with it?"

"But you're telling them you think it's an interesting program . . . right?"

"Right, but I still don't. . . ."

"How can they believe what you say when you look and sound so bored?"

"I do?"

"Your face looks like it was carved out of wood and your voice is an absolute monotone."

"It is *not*," George protested.

"Honey, I'm looking at you and listening to you. Come on, put some feeling into it. Pretend you're talking to Miss Waverly."

"Boy, you've got a memory like an elephant."

"And don't you forget it. Okay, again."

George went on. "We have heard from Mr. Zaynes about cars and from Mr. De Silva about roads. It is now my turn to talk to you. . . ."

"George. . . ."

"What have I done now?"

"It's what you haven't done. Your hands are hanging by your side like a couple of Polish sausages. When you say, 'It is now my turn to talk to you,' why don't you point to yourself? It's a natural gesture at that point, and it's effective."

George considered the suggestion. "Okay," he said, "but I'll forget it when I'm on my feet."

"Make a mark on the page, Dumbo. It'll help you remember."

"Oh, okay. Good idea. Here we go. . . . It is now *my* turn to talk to you . . ."

"Beautiful."

". . . about a business that makes it possible for Mr. Zaynes' cars to run on Mr. De Silva's roads after the sun goes down. With all due modesty, the Acme Lighting. . . ."

"Hey, hey! What was that?"

"What do you mean? You heard it, didn't you? With all due modesty, the Acme. . . ."

"You know what it sounded like, George? It sounded like you said, 'makes it possible for Mr. Zaynes' cars to run on Mr. De Silva's roads after the sun goes down with all due modesty' period. 'The Acme Lighting,' and so forth. Why did you pause after the word *modesty?*"

"I had to take a breath," George explained.

"Then take it after the word *down.* It needs a pause there anyway. And mark it so you won't forget."

"You don't do this sort of thing professionally, do you?" George asked.

"I'll ask for my fee later," Marge told him.

"You think I can afford it?"

"You'd better. No, not now, George. Business first."

"Okay," George grumbled, retreating to his place behind the bridge table they had set up.

"With all due modesty, the Acme Lighting Fixture Company's job is to shed some light on the activities that have just been described to us."

"Come on, George, you just made a funny. So smile. Let's see those pearlies."

"It's not that funny, Marge."

"No, it's not," Marge agreed. "But it's pleasant. They're not going to get the hiccups from laughing. But you know . . . maybe they'll smile. But they sure won't do it with you looking like a funeral director."

"All right, all right, Marge. . . . The Acme Lighting Fixture Company's job is to shed some light on the activities that have just been described to us. Ho! Ho! Ho!"

"George!" Marge's voice was sharp.

"What?"

"Is this a rehearsal or isn't it?"

"Yeah, sure, but. . . ."

"Then don't clown around. It's not going to do you any good at all if you don't work at it. You've got to imagine you're up on your feet at that luncheon, with the audience in front of you."

George felt a momentary stirring of uneasiness, but he brushed it off. "All right," he said. "I'll be serious. Of course, helping to shed light on the activities of this town is something that my company has been doing since 1925. I suppose I could list all the light poles we have supplied to Phillipsburg over the years."

"What's on that page, George, a *Playboy* centerfold?"

"What do you mean?"

"Whatever it is, you never take your eyes off it."

"Well, I'm reading it," George protested. "What do you want me to do, memorize it?"

"That'd be an act they'd remember. What would you do for an encore?"

"Hang myself. So what am I supposed to do?"

"Take in five or six words at a time. You can remember that much. Then look up while you're saying the phrase. No, not over my head. Right at me. Into my eyes."

"You're beautiful."

"George!"

"Okay, okay. But this is too much like work."

"I'll tell you what. Let's break the speech up into phrases. And make little slashes or whatever with a pencil. A bigger slash will be for a pause. And we'll underline certain words for emphasis. From the beginning again."

George sighed but did as he was told. "Good afternoon, ladies and gentlemen, and thank you, Mr. Benson. . . . Hey, Marge, how many times are we going to do this?"

"How many nights before the speech?"

"Six."

"Then we're going to do it six times."

George groaned, but squared his shoulders and started

again. "Good afternoon, ladies and gentlemen, and thank you, Mr. Benson. . . ."

XI

The food he had eaten was sitting in his stomach like a stone. George could feel his heart pounding in his chest and nothing seemed to ease his dry throat. He had long ago finished his own water and he didn't have the nerve to sneak his neighbor's. The funny thing was that he hadn't been nervous at all when he showed up for the luncheon, and this had pleased him. He had made friendly small talk with his luncheon mates and was actually looking forward to the main event.

But the minute Mr. Benson got to his feet and tapped his glass for order, that's when things began to tighten up. Through a fog, George heard Mr. Zaynes go on endlessly about the difference between the new and used car businesses, and he clapped with shaking hands when the man finished. And now it was Mr. De Silva's turn to talk about road building. It was pretty dull but it was long, and from George's point of view that was an unmixed blessing. The longer Mr. De Silva took, the more time he had to pull himself together. The trouble was, he wasn't doing it. He could feel the pieces coming unglued one by one. Finally, Mr. De Silva sat down. This time George didn't even bother to applaud. He couldn't lift his hands. For one awful moment, he thought he was going to lose his lunch. Then he realized he had to go to the bathroom. He simply *had* to go to the bathroom. As his eyes searched wildly for an escape route, he heard Mr. Benson pronounce the dreaded words, "And for our next speaker, it is my pleasure to present Mr. George Morris of Acme Lighting Fixture, which has been a fixture of this town for as long as any of us can remember."

He couldn't catch his breath. How could he talk if he

couldn't breathe? It was ridiculous. He couldn't get to the podium. He was paralyzed from the waist down. Why didn't the fools see that? What did they expect of a sick man?

"Mr. George Morris."

As the polite applause filled the room, George felt himself rise. He hadn't done it consciously, but there he was on his feet. And walking. That was amazing. And now he found himself standing in front of a lectern, and out front he could see several hundred hostile, sullen faces.

Somehow George managed a breath, and he heard someone say, "Good afternoon, ladies and gentlemen, and thank you, Mr. Benson."

It was him.

"I think your program chairman, Mr. Lasker, has put together a most interesting package for this meeting. We have heard from Mr. Zaynes about cars and from Mr. De Silva about roads. It is now my turn . . ."

Something was touching his chest, and George realized it was his own hand, pointing to himself on the word *my*, just as he and Marge had rehearsed it.

". . . to talk to you about a business that makes it possible for Mr. Zaynes' cars to run on Mr. De Silva's roads after the sun goes down."

Pause, dammit, he told himself. And then he heard a most remarkable sound. A gentle chuckle from the crowd. Not a belly laugh, but still a responsive stir.

"With all due modesty, the Acme Lighting Fixture Company's job is to shed some light on the activities that have just been described to us."

George smiled and looked up. To his utter astonishment, his audience was smiling back in encouragement. It dawned on George that this was not going to be so bad after all. He was not going to have to excuse himself to go to the men's room. In fact, he discovered that he rather liked being where he was. He settled in, and grooved his way right through to the end of his speech.

The applause he received was more than polite. It was appreciative and warm. After Mr. Benson had adjourned the meeting, Ed Lasker elbowed through the crowd around George and grabbed him by the hand.

"One of the best talks we've ever had, George. Thanks. Thanks a lot."

"Not at all, Ed," George grinned. "I was happy to do it."

"Ed? You're on a first-name basis with him?" The familiar voice belonged to Dandy Andy Durland. Andy's flower seemed a little wilted.

"Yes," George said. "He asked me to call him Ed."

"Oh," said Andy.

"George! I knew you'd do a hell of a job." It was Arthur Allers clapping him on the back.

"Thanks, Art. I enjoyed doing it."

"Guess who made it back in time for the luncheon?"

"Who?"

"Oscar Anderson. He had to leave for an appointment but he asked me to extend his congratulations."

"That's very nice of him."

"Hello, Mr. Allers." Somehow Andy Durland had managed to get himself between Allers and George. He was holding out his hand like a puppy. An uncertain smile flashed over Allers' face.

"Hello," he said. "I don't think I. . . ."

"This is Andy Durland, Art," George cut in promptly. "He's my boss."

"Oh. Of course, Durland. How are you? You've got a fine man there in George. A real comer."

Andy smiled weakly.

XII

"Sit down, George. . . ." Oscar Anderson indicated an armchair near his desk. "You know, you've raised quite a stir with that speech of yours. I don't know how many people at the chamber have called me up about it."

"Well, I'm . . . I'm glad," was all that George could think of to say.

"And Ed Lasker was especially impressed. He even gave me some free advice about you."

"What was that?"

"He told me that anybody who can handle himself on his feet as well as you did should be given a lot of responsibility."

"Oh?"

"Yes, and he gave me fair warning that if I didn't do something about it he was going to make you an offer to come to the bank."

"How did he know I'd come?"

Anderson laughed. "Good question. I asked him that, and he said he'd make you such a good offer you couldn't afford to turn it down. So I suppose I have to do something about you, for my own protection."

Here it comes, George thought to himself. I am going to get Dandy Andy's job.

"You know that Andy Durland's going to retire in a few months?"

George nodded.

"I've been wanting to restructure the department for some time now, and I think when he leaves is a good time to do it. You see, George, I'm overworked. This operation has gotten too big to run it all by myself. So what I've decided to do is this."

George held his breath.

"I've decided that Acme needs an assistant vice-president for finance, and you're going to be it."

"Me?" George practically yelped.

"That's right," Anderson said. "You'll be in line for my job when I leave. It's part of a new management philosophy to groom your own successor. What do you say, George? I warn you, it'll be a lot of hard work, but it'll mean another five hundred dollars a month to start with."

George's face must have reflected the incredulity he felt. "Five hundred!" he managed to blurt out.

"All right, George," Anderson said. "Make it six. You drive a hard bargain. Okay?"

"Okay," George said weakly.

"Why don't we have lunch today, and we can go over the details and the timing and so forth."

"Fine."

"In the meantime, my secretary can show you your new office. It's good to have you with me, George."

"It's good to be here . . . Oscar," George replied.

XIII

"And I'll be a mean, hard-driving boss. I'll claw my way to the top. I'll walk right over anybody who steps in my way. Why, I'll do anything. I'll even learn to play golf."

"You're going to neglect your family, right?"

"You bet."

George and Marge were sitting together on the sofa in their living room, laughing excitedly.

"You'll go off on long business trips and leave me behind."

"Right. Weeks and weeks at a time."

"And you'll call me at five o'clock to say you won't be home for dinner at all."

"No, I won't."

"You won't even call."

"Nope. I'll have my secretary call."

"Oh . . . you're going to get a secretary, too?"

"Sure."

"Any idea of who it's going to be?"

George looked at Marge seriously. "It's got to be somebody who's efficient and whose capabilities I know."

"Who's that?"

"Well, I thought . . . after all, we do owe her a favor, you know . . . I thought I'd ask Miss Waverly to leave the library. . . . Now Marge. Marge, stop it! I'll tickle you Marge. I promise you. . . ."

"George, now that's enough. George! For heaven's sake. What if Bobby should come in just now?"

"I'd make a speech," George murmured as he drew Marge slowly into his arms.

The Last Word

The fable you have just read naturally never happened, and probably never will. But it does serve to illustrate the point made earlier. Lightning can strike at any time. No matter what your job or profession, no matter what your interests, you are a candidate for a platform appearance. When it happens, don't panic. Think about the fundamental principles discussed in this book. They have been deliberately kept general because they constitute an approach to the solution of a particular problem rather than a specific prescription. You should have no trouble adapting them to your needs.

Remember, too, that dazzling oratory or a virtuoso performance is not expected of you. So don't set impossible standards for yourself. All that's required is a well-organized, clear statement of your views on whatever topic you select or are assigned. The three cardinal rules to remember are these —be logical, be simple, and be persuasive. And finally, be yourself.

If you can manage these, your audience will be relaxed and responsive. And who knows? Perhaps you will even find you enjoy speaking in public.